My Place
at
the Table

STORIES OF GOLF AND LIFE
BY LONGTIME
SPORTS COMMENTATOR

JOHN DERR

Published By
Old Sport Publishing
P.O. Box 1690
Pinehurst, North Carolina 28370
oldsport@nc.rr.com

Manufactured in the United States of America
by BookMasters
Ashland, Ohio, USA

Cover and content design by Tina Newell
Southern Pines, North Carolina, USA

Library of Congress Control Number: 2010907029

My Place
at
the Table

JOHN DERR

DEDICATED TO
PEGGY

WRITTEN FOR
CRICKET

CONTENTS

Introduction

John Derr is madly in love with my wife. And she feels pretty much the same about him. I've known about this "thing" for many years but, frankly, never thought it would lead to much since he's 50 years her senior—technically almost old enough to be her great- grandfather. John is either 92 or 93 years old, I forget which.

We've been friends and occasional golf partners for more than 15 years. Not long ago, despite an ailing eye Father Derr made a pair of monster cross-green birdies in an important team competition that cinched victory for his team. Indignant cries of a sandbagging Ninetysomething merely brought a rogueish smile from the birdie-making machine himself.

That's really what I most admire and love about John Derr. Not only does he possess one of the most agile and remarkable minds of any journalist I've ever known, but his ability to recall in the minutest detail stories and insights from an illustrious broadcasting career that really stretches from Ben Hogan's 1940 breakthrough at Pinehurst to the coming of Tiger Woods. This amounts to a one-man seminar on the golden age of the game.

That doesn't take into account his intimate conversations with Mahatma Gandhi during his years of military service in India. Nor of his close friendship with Grace Kelly, Arthur Godfrey, Red Barber and Edward R. Murrow, who hired him at CBS.

One of my favorite Derr tales concerns the November stroll on the golf course at Princeton when he was in town to broadcast the Dartmouth-Princeton Ivy League championship football game. He was introduced to Albert Einstein, who was out for his daily walk. The noted scientist confided to Derr that he feared the game of golf might be the most mentally perplexing sport ever played.

"If the smartest man who ever lived couldn't figure it out", Derr once declared to me over lunch on a sunny terrace, "what chance do the rest of us stand at mastering this game?"

All things being relative, John's life and times seem to possess a wonderful quality of pure serendipity, the result of an incredibly upbeat case of Newspaper Curiosity that has caused him to brush up against and befriend many of the most compelling and important figures of the past century, particularly in the world of golf.

Not surprisingly, Derr was the only reporter Ben Hogan thought enough of to invite him to walk every step of his farewell triumph at Carnoustie in 1953, Byron Nelson turned to him for guidance in broadcasting and Sam Snead liked to travel with him so much Derr became a trusted friend and confidant.

I am thrilled to report that you'll encounter

many of these remarkable people and much more in the pages of this extended volume of John Derr's collected musings and writings. You'll find a witty and often touching final stroke of the pen from one of the most endearing characters -- and remarkable journalism careers -- of all time. I am proud to call John Derr not only a friend, but one of my heroes, for he set the gold standard of journalism that many of us are still hoping to someday achieve.

Meantime, I just wish the ageless Derr's golf game would show some signs of giving in to the verdict of time or at least show some respect for Old Man Par. Otherwise my wife, Wendy, is likely to run off with the sandbagging Ninetysomething.

PROLOGUE

During the decades I was reporting sports in newspapers, magazines, books, early radio, television and speaking to church groups and civic clubs and just telling stories, I enjoyed a lifetime that most folks would have given away the farm to have shared.

Just color me lucky.

These experiences brought me face to face with many well-known athletes and world figures. It has been my pleasure to share many memories of them --- memories (some good and some bad) seen and reported from **My Place at the Table**. Where was the table? The table was at any media location on the front row, courtside, ringside, trackside or in a radio or television booth, 20 feet above the fairway.

Hindsight is something I should have thought of yesterday. It would be great if we could conduct our lives like we repair mistakes on our computer--- punch a button and restore life as it was. Too late in my career I realized I had never bothered to collect autographs or photographs of athletes with or without me in the picture. What I did retain were memories of my relationship with these people whom I call friends. It was after having heard me recall some memories that my daughter, Cricket, insisted I should put on paper some of these episodes. It was for her that I did, about 100. And now I want you to share some of these with us, some new and others you've asked me to repeat.

It may not have occurred to you that athletics or sports can be a most credible portrait of conduct in one's life. As I have closely observed those who compete in sports, it serves as a barometer of the kind of person a man or lady is likely to be in living their life. The very word -- sports- - to most of us means a leisurely endeavor, enjoyed with friends or friendly foes. Regardless of the sport, one rule fits all. Play hard. Play fair. Play to win.

I've heard of companies, who when hiring new personnel, followed a plan of having applicants play golf with staff officers, believing conduct on the golf course can be a predictable measure of one's worthiness. Cheating in sports is easier to detect. Good sportsmen are most often good sports.

Understand these stories are not biographies. This is a recollection of how I knew these people, sometimes for only a few minutes, others for a lifetime. Some will be revealed differently than you might have believed. Most stars have two personalities – one very private and the other public. It may appear that I liked everybody in sports. That was not true. However as a reporter, I had to surrender my right to be a fan. Most of the time.

In this project I have recalled for Cricket and

you, some whose character showed me a side of them I was pleased to adopt. I observed all the people I met, always looking for ways to improve my own performance, to learn from those wiser than I. That's a good habit. I can truthfully say I learned from everyone I ever met, if it was only to smile while I was hurting.

There were a few open spaces on some pages. I don't like to waste paper. I had a few jokes I wanted to use but the warden wouldn't let me. But since I've made a career of hunting birdies, a covey of birds have been scattered through the pages. This prevents you from having to hear my blow-by-blow description of the 128 yard ace I made on Arnie's Mid South club, two weeks before my 92nd birthday. Some day, I must tell you about it. In the meantime, enjoy the birdies, drawn especially for you.

If we don't learn from those who have led the way, we forfeit an opportunity to make our lives more enjoyable and meaningful. Any coach will tell you that forfeits are something to be avoided.

Enough of the serious stuff, come meet some of my friends.

During the late summer of 1974 the sounds of hammers, buzzing electric saws and creaking concrete mixers were heard at Pinehurst, NC, as dozens of workmen hurried to complete the $2.5 million World Golf Hall of Fame. It was scheduled to open on September 11 and that date was fast approaching.

The multi-columned Hall of Fame building, a tribute to the game of golf as recognized around the world sat serenely in the pines of North Carolina, looking all the while as if it had been transferred there from some Grecian forestland. It would be ready but the main speaker was not yet set. With 'divine assistance' this is how the dedicatory speaker was obtained.

This was about the time when everything in Washington was in monumental disarray. Our vice president had been returned to private life. A Michigan congressman had been drafted to fill the vacancy of the vice presidency. The natives grew wildly restive. For the first time a sitting president of the United States would become a standing ex-president as Richard Nixon flew to his nest in the West. It was a time when long range, or even short range plans were difficult. And the WGHF had plans to make.

Meanwhile, back in Pinehurst, an international project as important as the golf shrine needed a major world figure to cut the ribbon. Don Collett, president of the WGHF, had hoped to get Pres. Nixon, He was only a so-so golfer but loved the game. He had actually scored a hole-in-one while he was in the White House. Mr. Nixon was invited but was too busy to respond. And so the invitation was sent to the new vice president, Gerald Ford. There was no acceptance from him either. Were they not getting our mail, the USPO snail mail at that time?

Mr. Ford was pretty busy too but we needed a big name. After all, in a few weeks we would be inducting into the Hall the greatest living golfers in the world. Coming to Pinehurst were Ben Hogan, Sam Snead, Byron Nelson, Patty Berg and the current 'big three' Jack Nicklaus, Arnold Palmer and Gary Player, all marquee names.

As a congressman, Rep. Ford, longtime friend of Jim Kemper, always came to Charlotte to play the Kemper Pro-Am event. This preceded the regular Kemper, but now as the Veep his plans may have changed. There was late confirmation that he was going to play. On the day of the Pro-Am I drove to Charlotte with Don's invitation letter in my pocket. Since we had not reached Mr. Ford in Washington, I said let's go to Plan A. Catch him at the Kemper.

Having televised the Kemper several times I knew my way around the Quail Hollow clubhouse. Maybe by dusting off my CBS /PGA badge I could hang out in the locker room until Mr. Ford changed his shoes. I nearly got through but the Secret Service didn't pay much attention to my badge and they kept shoving me away.

I gave up on Plan A and the locker room. My next stop was the putting green, it was more accessible to me. I would begin Plan B.

Soon Mr. Ford, putter in hand, joined the other contestants to stroke a few putts. He was relaxed as he moved his way around the putting green, chatting with some of the other competitors and seemingly in a good frame of mind. That was to my advantage. Then he came toward my side of the putting green. Now I could get closer to him but every time I moved closer the Secret Service agents emphatically suggested I move back.

Frustrated, I had no choice.
Plan B. was not working.
This meant Plan C.

Plan A was the locker room and it had not worked. I had gone through Plan B., alongside the putting green. It almost worked but it was obvious I was not going to be able to talk with Mr. Ford personally. I was going to need a messenger, someone to actually hand the letter to Mr. Ford. A ha !

A long ago requested 'miracle' was about to happen. Standing in front of me was Dr. Billy Graham, putting his way over to my side of the green. This Charlotte native, the great evangelist, often played at the Kemper and I was delighted to see him. I had found my messenger.

With my friendliest smile, I beckoned to him. The Secret Service, still eyeing me, would not interfere with the Reverend. He used a higher grade Protector. Re-introducing myself, I quickly explained my mission and my need of his help.

I wanted to get that letter to Mr. Ford. I had been unable to do so in Washington, and so far I wasn't doing too well in Charlotte. The Hall was very much interested in having Vice President Ford as the speaker at the dedication and induction ceremonies.

Dr. Graham understood my problem, took the letter and quickly stepped across the practice green. I watched him explain to Mr. Ford why he was playing postman. The VP learned he was being invited to dedicate the World Golf Hall of Fame. Dr. Graham projected that Mr. Ford would spend a memorable day with all those famous golfers in Pinehurst. After learning the news and hearing Dr. Graham's enthusiastic explanation, Mr. Ford turned toward me across the green, put up his thumbs ..... Signaling okay.

Very simple, once you get to the right man, in this case the right man was-- Dr. Billy Graham, whom I first met months before at a golf course in the Caribbean. That chance meeting at the Iron Shore Country club in Jamaica turned out to be significant. Through it I had established a face on relationship with the great American evangelist. This was enough to let me ask Dr. Graham to deliver the WGHF invitational letter. Carry the mail.

Meeting the Reverend in Montego Bay had not been by design. My wife, Peggy, and I were in Jamaica on holiday and were finishing our golf for that day. I went into the locker room and there, facing the wall and mirror, I noticed my neighbor was Dr. Graham, a friend of many presidents. I was nonplussed when he greeted me by name saying "Hello, John. Are you down here on a golfing holiday?"

He must have noticed I was shocked at his recognition.

"Oh, yes. I watch some TV golf programs and I'm familiar with your work. I watch when it's convenient and occasionally on Sunday I see your interview with the winner."

Several staff members were with him and they invited us to watch them play the first hole. Dr. Graham's second shot was a good one, reaching the front of the green but 30 feet short of the hole. A few minutes later I thought it sacrilegious when a Graham staff member yelled: "Come on, Billy. Show us a miracle." I was embarrassed by that but I learned it was okay to ask for a miracle.

Dr. Graham failed to hole the long putt, so there was no "miracle" on that Jamaica green that day. However that chance meeting at the golf club would be most helpful months later on the putting green at Charlotte. It secured the speaker to handle the dedication of the World Golf Hall of Fame at Pinehurst.

Billy Graham's delayed "miracle" arrived. That's why President Ford was on hand to dedicate the golf shrine at Pinehurst in 1974. Actually, I think it was the chance to mingle with Hogan, Snead, Nelson, and the Young Turks that got us our speaker -- but there was no better time to use the Reverend's miracle.

"Golf is no funeral, though - both can be sad affairs."

-Bob Jones, 1946

It was my good fortune to have lived during the middle of the twentieth century when, even without the benefit of television, America produced a number of sports heroes who were bigger than life. A myriad of sports writers helped make it so. These were great athletes, judged by their performances.

One such hero was Robert Tyre Jones, Jr., of Atlanta, GA, known to an admiring public as Bobby Jones, but known to his friends simply as Bob, the name he favored after his youthful days. If you ever encounter someone who tells you he was a good friend of Bobby Jones, look with askance on that friendship.

The records Jones set in golf, the tournaments he won and his dominance of the world golf scene for two decades are all available in record books. They will not be dealt with here.

Spend a few moments of personal recall of Jones, the man. It was at the second Masters (1935) that as a young sports writer I met him. Grantland Rice, the best known sports writer of that era, whom I had met the day before, asked if I had met Mr. Jones. When I said I hadn't, Mr. Rice, himself a charming, kindly soul, found an opportunity to introduce me.

A friendship begun that day continued throughout his life. Through that acquaintanceship many doors were opened for me and many important sports heroes were met. I never knew why Bob "took a liking" to me but I respected him being my friend.

Some years later Bob was being given an award by the Metropolitan Golf Writers Association in a New York hotel, and prior to the dinner I was visiting with him in the reception room. As we were talking, a large, graying man, with the look of an old athlete written in his manner of walking, came across the room to our side of the hall.

"Do you recognize that fellow?" Jones asked me.

I didn't.

By that time he had reached us, obviously coming to greet the honored guest.

"Shake hands with Ty Cobb." Bob's simple introduction...So typical of Jones' thoughtfulness, this kind, caring man. As the two sons of Georgia exchanged pleasantries, I couldn't help but think how different were these two dominant sportsmen, each recognized as the best in his field...one universally loved and one whose great career had generated intense hatred.

Twice I had the thrill of having Jones ask me to lend him my good right arm. The first time was at the funeral of his good friend, Grantland Rice.

Bob was an honorary pallbearer, one of many. He had come to New York for the funeral, even though his crippling illness already hindered his walking unattended.

That he asked my help in walking up the aisle thrilled me. Another pallbearer would have been pleased to lend him an arm and that star-studded procession read like a Who's Who. Among them were Jack Dempsey, Gene Tunney, Eddie Arcaro, Red Blaik, Casey Stengel, Bill Corum, Red Barber, Ted Husing, Elmer Layden, Don Budge and Hank Greenberg.

They were all all-time greats, except for the young lad on whose right arm Jones laboriously made his way up the aisle.

The other time he asked me to lend him an arm was at Golf House in Manhattan where the USGA was unveiling the likeness of Jones that had been painted by President Eisenhower. It was such a simple act, to assist him to the dais, but to be at his side in this impressive moment of his career was rewarding.

True, I was only his "aisle caddie" but he was My Man.

Once at Augusta National, not at tournament time, I sat on the verandah with Jones and asked him at what point was he most nervous in a competition.

"Does it begin to get to you when you are about the 16th hole with a lead that you don't want to slip away?" I asked.

"Oh, no. The last few holes are not time for nervousness. If you are playing well there's no need to get nervous. However, you are apt to get quicker or stronger and you have to guard against over-clubbing. Your adrenalin is so high that often you have to back off from a six to a seven iron.

"Nervousness? I was nervous going to the first tee in every round of every match I played in competition. I never concerned myself about the ability of others. I knew they could play, but I did wonder about my own game. You probably won't believe this but I was nervous every time, wondering if I might whiff the ball. I was that nervous.

"My knees would be knocking, I was so unsure of what might happen on the first tee. I often wondered if people could hear or see them. If I had worn plus fours (a la Sarazen) they could not have seen them but they might have heard them. I think they were playing "Dixie" by the time I put the tee in the ground.

"After that first tee, no. It was done with."

For the first dozen or more years of CBS television coverage of the Masters, beginning in 1956, one of my assignments was to dash up from the 15th green location to the Butler Cabin alongside the clubhouse. There I would introduce Jones and Mr. Roberts for the ceremony honoring the winner, putting on the green jacket and all.

If I ran fast enough I could sit with Jones as we watched the closing holes on a monitor. Often he would have meaningful comments about the play and players.

It was during this interval at the 1965 tournament when Jack Nicklaus was spread-eagling the field that Jones turned from the monitor and made his oft-quoted evaluation – perhaps the greatest praise ever accorded Jack's game—"Nicklaus is playing a game of which I am not familiar."

Jones was not speaking for immortality. He was voicing an opinion from his own background of excellence.

Jones was a man of unusual skills and unlimited vision. In the fall of 1955 we were touring the Augusta National course in a station wagon, surveying where cameras should be located for the television coverage the next April.

"We may as well determine locations on all 18 holes," Jones told the CBS TV crew. "They are not doing it yet, but one of these days television will cover all 18 holes."

This was a time when cameras covered only the last three or four holes. No one dared think of covering all 18, the logistics being so primitive. But Jones foresaw that day.

He was more than just a golfer. That may have been one of his lesser traits; he worked at it less than some others. He was an engineer, a lawyer, an author, and an administrator. He was a traditionalist but at the same time an innovator.

I was fortunate to have him as a friend, encouraging me to keep looking ahead, trying to improve my profession, saying uphill was easier, if the goal was in view. He helped me understand competitive golf and made my reporting more factual, and hopefully more interesting. His suggestions were always to the point, never cruel, always helpful.

Jones never tried to improve my playing – that was too much of a challenge, even for Jones. But with his help I became a better reporter and broadcaster of his sport.

Born on St. Patrick's Day in 1902, Jones died at the age of 69, one week before Christmas in 1971.

We knew the end was near, blessedly so, for he had suffered valiantly those final months. When I got the call that Jones had died I immediately went to my home club and requested the membership flag be lowered to half-staff.

"What member died?" the attendant asked.

Sadly I informed him it was the great Bob Jones. That man in Atlanta should be considered a member – an honored member, not an honorary member – at this and every other club where golf is played. So it was, signaling universal sorrow, the flag flew in mourning until his funeral.

(Cricket, you never knew this great man, nor he you, but he cared for you. That's why, when

you were born, there was a hand-written letter, saying he hoped to be on hand to see you crowned champion in 1976. He died five years earlier.)

As we walked away from the green at the short No. 6 hole of Pinehurst's No. 2 course, a day that had been overcast and gray silently became alive with micro-snowflakes fluttering down. The winter rye grass on the dogleg seventh hole was taking on a white cover, pristine white.

"Mr. Tufts, it looks as though your thermal belt has slipped South," my newly-acquired Yankee bride, Peggy, jabbed at our playing companion, Richard Tufts, president and major domo of the celebrated golfing mecca of the Carolinas. I cringed. You don't jab Mr. Tufts at Pinehurst. It was Peggy's first meeting with the man affectionately known throughout golfdom as "Mister Richard," a man she later came to love as I did.

"Peggy, surely you're not going to let a few duck feathers ruin your golf game. This is merely a shower, nothing serious and the sun will be out before we finish. A little snow doesn't upset a Yankee, does it?"

"No sir," she answered, heeding my frown, begging her to respect our host. "I've been a member of the Ski Patrol for 6 years. Let it snow." She would play through the snow, it was only that she had recently been told, in glowing terms by me and others, that the trade winds of the Caribbean drifted inland and formed a warmer thermal belt through the Carolina Sandhills. And it was true, most of the time. Really.

Richard Tufts, a man of sturdy New England stock, was born in 1896, a year after his grandfather, James W. Tufts, purchased 6,000 acres of pineland in the Sandhills. The elder Mr. Tufts paid a dollar an acre for the property. The former owner thought he had found a sucker who'd pay that much for his barren wasteland. The business man from Massachusetts clearly considered it a bargain, and so it was. This acreage would one day be home to one of America's earliest sports, health and golf resorts of the 19th century.

When Mr. Richard succeeded his father to head the family operation, Pinehurst moved to the forefront of golf venues. Donald Ross came from Scotland with his brother, Alex, and taught the game to hundreds. Ross gained international fame as an architect, leaving his designs on hundreds of courses, many of which still proudly claim their Ross parentage. As Mr. Richard managed his New England-like fiefdom, he welcomed a few home owners, developed tournaments that attracted the best players from across the land and enhanced the reputation of Pinehurst. Together Ross and Tufts made a formidable combination.

Early golf courses often did not include practice grounds until the Tufts-Ross combine came up with "maniac hill", where golfers could go to practice and not interfere with those who were trying to play the course. Prior to that all lessons and practice took place while sharing the regular holes near the clubhouse.

The innovation of a place to practice, the new tournaments he established, and his system to equalize playing abilities through an improved handicap system were considered by many to be Richard Tufts' biggest legacy. Others, including many USGA colleagues gave greater credit to his dedication to codifying golf's equitable rules of play. He was not just a "rules expert". He wrote the rules. His sense of fairness was astounding. In 1951 he was the chief architect during extended consultations with the Royal and Ancient officials in establishing conforming rules of the game.

Richard Tufts, a shy man whose quietness was always seen as thoughtfulness and never indifference, left his notable fingerprints on everything that had to do with the game of golf. As a course owner, he provided the playing fields. He supported new competitions that brought players to his venues. As an arbiter of rules, he was steady in invoking the value of equity for all. He did not think rules penalized players. Penalties were self-incurred and avoidable. Trained in Harvard to plan ahead, as he became more active administratively in golf, Mr. Tufts accepted increasing responsibility with the national organization. He came up through the ranks and served as Chairman of all seven major operating committees of the USGA. The first to do so.

Mr. Tufts was President of the USGA in 1956

and 1957, years in which golf enjoyed increased popularity. An appreciative roster of amateur golfers, especially juniors and ladies enjoyed the new USGA competitions. Golf's governing body was never better administered, said his colleagues.

It's appropriate to mention here that Mr. Tufts, who counted many golf professionals as close personal friends did not exude love for the PGA. Early on, before the Tour became all powerful, Pinehurst hosted the North and South Open each year. The professionals were complimentary guests at Pinehurst's own Carolina hotel. For free. The midweek purse was smaller than some, understandably, but the PGA wanted to change the deal. Pinehurst was asked to forgo free room and board, and add equivalent cash to the purse.

Pinehurst had more rooms and meals than it had cash and the deal stood. As a result the North and South Open was scratched from the schedule. At the time it was rated no lower than 4th among all professional tournaments. The 1940 North and South was Ben Hogan's first win on the tour. Now gone.

One could say his Revision of the Rules Book was Tufts' greatest contribution to the sport he loved and nurtured. Sometimes, however, you have to decide what is fair, without a Rules Book. I recall once Mr. Tufts was asked what was his most unusual ruling. And this is what he told me:

"My first year on the Rules Committee, I

was assigned to officiate the semi-final round of the Amateur championship. Two great players, great friends, were paired. I started the match. Each drove well. Each played approach shots into the same bunker, close together. I asked them to identify their ball. Both were playing the same brand. Each was using a No. 4, their ID markings were nearly the same.

"Here I had two indistinguishable balls, buried in the sand. One in an easy location, much better than the other. Who was who? Neither could identify his ball, an error. Penalizing both was no help. So I told them to collect their balls, we were returning to the first tee and starting over. Use different markings this time. They did and the match went fine.

"I understand some of the USGA veterans, watching down the first hole said…. 'Look out there at Tufts. He's gone only one hole and he's bringing them in already.' Equity dictated my choice, and I used it."

Mr. Tufts considered two major tenets. (1) Play the course as you find it, no bending of limbs or improving the lie, and (2) Put your ball in play and do not touch it until you withdraw it from the hole. With that as his guide, there were no ties, no ifs, no ands or no buts.

A personal observation: In 1938, while working at the Greensboro Daily News, I became a victim of exhaustion, fell in my apartment bath room, hit my head and was out of it. When my twice- a- week maid let herself in the room to begin her chores, she may have thought I was dead. She sounded the alarm and I was carted away to the hospital. Rest a few weeks was the order of the doctor. Meanwhile, no driving. Lots of walking. Rest. Eat. Rest.

After a note explaining my absence appeared on the sports page, Mr. Tufts called the newspaper and suggested that I be brought to the Carolina hotel in Pinehurst for my rehab. This sounded like a good idea. Offer accepted.

A neat room on the 3rd floor was home. Mr. Tufts stopped by one day, inquiring about my health. Recovery was going well and I told him I was being picked up the next day. I was going back to Greensboro. Back to work.

"Have you played No. 2 on this trip?" Mr.Tufts asked.
"No sir. I haven't. But I won't have time now."
"Oh, yes, you will. I'll call the paper and tell them. I think you should stay right here at the hotel until you are recovered enough to play No. 2."

What else could I do? A fitting punishment in rehab, thank you.

From Babe Didrickson Zaharias I learned a new meaning of courage, hope, honesty, and kindness.

Her exploits as an athlete have been well chronicled, although many of today's sports fans never had the opportunity to exult over her achievements.

The 1932 Olympics belonged to her. You can look it up. She had come out of a small Texas school to be a one-woman track team and single-handedly a winner for her school over other fully-manned teams.

After her Olympic brilliance she tried her hand at softball, baseball, tennis and golf and showed superior skill in each. Eventually it was golf that held her attention.

She regained her amateur status after a brief fling as a professional, sailed across the Atlantic and captured the championship of Great Britain. It was there she told reporters who asked how she could power the ball so long and so straight that Babe told them she "just loosened my girdle and let it fly."

Soon afterwards she turned professional again and with her friend and rival, Patty Berg, was the moving force in organizing an association of lady professionals.

Another group attempted to organize the

lady pros but without Babe and Patty it was doomed. The public was confused about the growing controversy between the two fledgling groups.

One day Babe was competing at the Palma Cia club in Tampa. As she walked by the scorer's tent I spoke to her, introduced myself and asked if I could talk with her a few minutes before she left the club. She agreed.

As she came out of the clubhouse twenty minutes later she bolted over to me and asked, "Do you think I'm losing my mind?"

"No. Certainly not. Why do you ask?"

"Well you came up to me and said... 'I'm John Derr from CBS.' All the time I was taking my shower I tried to figure why you had said that. He must think I've lost my memory or my mind. I've known you a long time."

"Yes, I know, but you meet so many people and I want to ask you some questions and be able to quote you that I wanted to be sure you realized to whom you were talking."

Babe looked at me with that smile that started with the upturned corners of her mouth and carried through to her brown eyes. "Don't worry. I consider you a friend and know when I can trust a friend. What did you want to ask?"

The answers she gave I don't remember, but I've never forgotten that affirmation of friendship from a true star.

Cancer knocked down the Babe but it didn't knock her out. She suffered through months of treatment and we all thought that brilliant career was finished. We would never again hear the enthusiastic applause when she strode to the first tee.

But we were wrong. She showed great courage and determination. As her strength returned she started chipping and putting. And then we heard she was hitting wood shots.

Husband George Zaharias was a professional wrestler, one of the famous Zaharias brothers in the world of grunt and groan. Big George adored the Babe and he tenderly coaxed her back to health. She was playing golf but not playing tournaments.

Then the next winter she entered the Serbin Open at the Bay Shore club on Miami Beach. Most of the world's best players were there. Not until the last nine did the Babe figure to be a factor. Three quick birdies moved her up and she roared home a winner, a most popular victory.

There was no television, no radio. I was there to get a report for my Sunday night radio program. In those days CBS did not allow tape recordings to be broadcast. Every word was live.

As Babe came out to the putting green where three or four hundred fans waited to see her receive her trophy and check, I stopped her and asked if she could appear live with me on the 10:30 program.

"Let's talk about it later," she said and at that moment a club official called to say she had a long distance phone call from George in Tampa.

Babe turned and went to take the call. The crowd waited.

After a few minutes the Babe re-appeared and in the earshot of the several hundred fans she called to me. She had a flair for the dramatic and I always suspected she anticipated the reaction her comment would get from those around the green.

"John, I can't do your show. That was George on the phone. Good old George. He knew I would win again. He said for me to come right home, he has a prize for me. And I want to get there before it goes down."

You don't comment on that, just let it drift on.

Babe's great courage proved not enough. Once more cancer struck and this time it was the winner.

On the Saturday of the 1956 Masters tournament I was called to a phone in the press center. It was less than 15 minutes before I was scheduled to voice another report, but when I learned it was Zaharias I took the call.

"I've been listening to CBS," she said, from her hospital bed, "and I want you to tell Hogan and Nelson and Mangrum and Demaret that this old Texas gal is still pulling for the Texans."

After assuring her they would get the message and with one eye on the clock we chatted a minute. Then I remembered the Sports Broadcasters Association had recently voted her the outstanding female athlete of the century. She was to receive the honor in New York in September.

"I've got to run now, but I'll see you in New York when we give you your medal," in closing the call.

Then this poignant response.

"No, John, I won't see you in New York. This time it's got me. I wanted to tell you what it has meant to be your friend. But this is goodbye. I won't be speaking with you again."

In about four minutes I did my Masters update, tears falling freely.

In a few months, the Babe died.

It had been only 10 years since Johnny Goodman. In 1933, stood quietly among the late afternoon crowd surrounding the 18th green at the North Shore Country club near Chicago, clutching in his small hands the USGA Open trophy. Victory by an amateur was being celebrated by surprised fans who thought if an amateur would win it had to be the man from Atlanta, Robert Tyre Jones.

Not so. Unheralded Johnny Goodman had defeated all the professionals in our country's most prestigious event!

But now it was 1943, ten years later and seemed like 100, so much had happened in that decade of time. A depression had passed and a war had come. Like thousands of other Americans Goodman had traded his spikes for Army boots and instead of the cheers of golf fans his ears were attuned to the bark of a drill sergeant. Instead of North Shore's luxurious verdancy, here were the dusty sands, mountains, and hot nights of Northern India.

"Look what I've got." Private Goodman literally yelled, as he charged into my office at CBI Theater Headquarters in New Delhi, holding a white oblong envelope. The front was marked like a practicing doodler had been at work. Addresses were marked through. Another had been written, scratched out and yet another written. The mailmen in some way had forwarded this letter from several out of date Army addresses on two sides of the world until it reached its APO destination.

"It's my invitation to the Masters, " beamed Johnny, "and now they've called it off."

Enclosed in the formal invitation was a small card from Clifford Roberts announcing the 1943 Masters had been canceled, due to "world conditions" as I remember the wording.

There was to be no Masters for Goodman or anyone else that year or the next two since "world conditions" did not improve to normal until the 1946 renewal at Augusta. There was however golf for the great little Omaha golfer as he spent many off-duty hours at the Royal Gymkhana Golf course in Old Delhi. The patriotic warrior used his duty time off doing what he did well - golf.

Goodman was a good tee shot player, not long even by the standards of that day but he was seldom out of position. Occasionally when he tried for distance, look out for the big hook but when he paced his swing it was smooth and straight as one could want. His short game was exceptional and there were many rounds when his putts totaled less than 30, despite the conditions of the Indian greens.

In those days Johnny, who had also won the US Amateur championship in 1937 had no idea of turning pro although many years later

I think he did give up his amateur status to become the professional at a club in California. His willingness to impart his knowledge to others made him a doubly popular player to be sought for a game. This was true not only of the American enlisted men and officers but there were frequent occasions in which he would be "requested" to play with Gen. Sir Archibald Wavell, the then Viceroy of India and an avid golfer and a good one. Handicap once a 2, but I saw him often. He was not that good.

On more than one afternoon Goodman would call and tell me our date was off ... "The Viceroy wants to play today," No other explanation was needed. RHIP and if there is some civilian who doesn't understand.... that famed acronym means:

Rank Has Its Privileges.

One-day Goodman asked if I thought we could get enough players together to have an Indian version of the Walker Cup. He spent about a month checking the games of American golfers stationed in New Delhi who might passably represent the USA. Once assured that he had a competitive team Goodman confirmed the matches to Gen. Wavell and a date was set. A marvelous Indian sportsman, H. M. Malik, his ebony beard partially covered by his white turban was an outstanding golfer and was matched against Goodman. Another opponent was Lieut. Robert Neil, of Glasgow, who had won the Scottish Closed championship at St. Andrews in the last outing there before the war. He was a Plus 2 handicap, and played to it. India also used a local band leader, who is remembered for two idiosyncrasies: One, he hired 3 caddies for his round. One to look for the ball. (If available golf balls cost $5). Caddie No. 2 was trustworthy and was hired to make sure the first caddie didn't pocket the balls. No. 3 was really No. 1 but not under the caste system. He had two jobs – to carry the bag of clubs and – immediately before the stroke --- to remind the piano player, "Keep your head down."

He was permitted these extra assistants during Goodman's Walker Cup, but why not? The Viceroy was accompanied by six gun-toting body guards, two caddies for similar duty and a committee, dressed in sparkling white garb, appearing ready to ward off the monkeys who overran the course and absconded with an occasional ball. Under Johnny's rules, Lord Wavell had no limit on ball watchers, although I never heard them cheer his good shots.

As I recall the outcome, the USA won the match by a couple of points but no history books record the match or the outcome. What was important then and decades later was the enthusiasm generated by golfers from widely differing backgrounds which could result in a wartime diversion of friendly combat on such a pleasant field so far from homes. Goodman's spirit of competition made it possible.

Goodman's capture of the Open, coming only three years after the end of Bob Jones' domination, was not as surprising in 1933 as it might seem to be. There had been no time interval to permit writers to ponder the possibility of an amateur winning the Open title again after the reign of Mr. Jones.

Muscular Frank Stranahan and Harvie Ward, as amateurs were good enough to win but neither did. And soon the appeal of professional competition caused many good players to quit the amateur ranks. Jones wanted an amateur to win at Augusta and some day one might but the last amateur to capture our Open championship was Johnny Goodman in 1933.

Not having seen Goodman's triumph by a slim stroke over Ralph Guldahl in 1933 but having heard he was a brash, cocky little scrapper I once asked him if his cockiness had made him a better player.

"I never considered myself cocky, if you mean I was a showoff bragging player. People may have mistaken confidence for cockiness. Yes, I was a confident player most of the time but I don't think anyone can play good golf unless he has a big share of confidence. When I was playing a lot (inferring that his good playing days might have ended) I've played with a lot of confidence and you can't win any other way," Goodman averred.

Asked how he retained that confidence for 72 holes in the Open he won, Goodman gave me an answer which I remember clearly. 50 years later.

"Confidence is built on repeated success

and the memory of success. If I miss the putt I try to forget that stroke immediately. Never store up memories of the shots that fail. Only the ones that work, remember those. And one other thing that helped me was I never changed my style or pace of play. A lot of people go through different pre-stroke routines if they face a putt which they feel is a 'must make'. That is a bad habit. I never felt it helped me to delay stroking a putt after I once had settled on the line and speed. Any extra looking doesn't help and may hurt. Uncertainty is an enemy of confidence."

Somewhere on the back nine Goodman lost a little of his confidence, he admitted. "There was a putt dead center that I knew was perfect, but it skipped across the rim and two feet beyond. But it was perfect." (Who hasn't felt that?)
Or he may have been looking behind him. The pros were charging.

Goodman balanced an opening 76 with a brilliant 66 in the second round. His 70 in round three pushed him in front, with a little margin, all of which he needed. At the end of 72, Johnny bettered Guldahl's 288 by a single stroke. Walter Hagen, after a horrible start, came to life in the last round, posting a 66, ten better than Johnny on that day, but when it was over, it was the amateur who was crowned America's No 1 golfer.

Goodman was excited, brimming with confidence despite possibly a few anxious moments on the closing holes that day in Chicago. Cheering by appreciative fans was something new for this little known amateur. Even though he may not have been cocky with hat in hand as he accepted the trophy, he thought nothing better could ever match that moment.

I wasn't there in 1933, but when his Masters invitation followed him to far-away India, one could sense a surge in renewed confidence. His elation was real. No crowds. No cheers. None needed. Just two GI buddies enjoying a bono moment for both.

He again was Johnny Goodman, US Open champion. His audience was one. A cancelled invitation had re-ignited his Nebraska confidence.

Bring 'em on, bring 'em on.

When you find yourself sharing the same bay in a locker room with the former King of England and you are a reporter, you begin to wonder how you can get him to do an interview.

This happened at the Greenbrier Hotel in White Sulphur Springs, in the early 50's, during the Sam Snead Festival, a pro-am honoring the Greenbrier professional.

Lockers were assigned on arrival and since I had stopped by on my way back to New York from the Kentucky Derby, I was on hand Monday evening. The next morning an attendant took me to the third bay of the locker room and I began to change into my golf shoes.

Within a few minutes there was a hubbub in that bay as several men, among them the Duke of Windsor, walked by. Most of them were hotel executives. The Duke had been assigned the locker three down the aisle from mine.

Respecting the ex-King's privacy, as soon as I had changed shoes I left the locker room and the dignitaries. But an idea was taking place. Not since his abdication and wedding to Mrs. Simpson had the Duke been interviewed on American radio.

On Saturday I would originate my CBS sports news show from the Greenbrier and I wanted the Duke as my guest. But how?

His newly published biography, *A King's Story*, had just been released and although you wouldn't want to call it a promotional appearance, I knew his publishers would welcome it.

You don't just walk up to a King or even an ex-King and ask him to go on a broadcast with you. I chased down Snead, who was friendly with Windsor and had played with him a few times. Sam said the best way was to broach the subject with his equerry and let him explain what I had in mind. This I was able to do, as the equerry was approachable.

Initially he thought it unlikely, but I explained my questions would be confined to golf and his new book, as I had no interest in social or political matters. It could be done by phone in the locker room and would take only five minutes.

He said he would mention it to the Duke later.

Friday the equerry said on two conditions the Duke would consider it. Not that he would do it, but would consider it. I was to submit the questions for his approval and the telephone interview would have to originate in his hotel suite. The Duke did not want on-lookers or eavesdroppers around. No problem.

Along with others in our bay we had been casually introduced earlier in the week, but not until Saturday morning did I feel confident the broadcast would take place. CBS Press information in New York had been notified and they had issued a release with the news that the first post-abdication interview would be heard Saturday at 6:30 on my CBS Radio show.

When I came into his suite, he appeared more nervous that a man facing a downhill putt on an icy slick green. Me, too.

The interview went as outlined. As these things go, this was not much of an interview, very forgettable. For me the highlight had come at the close when I said, "Thank you, Sir."

He offered his hand and said, "You're welcome, John."

The ex-King had called me by name.

Sam Snead caused me my biggest problem in my reportorial career – in print and on the air.

When I became a professional reporter my first editor impressed upon me the fact that I had forfeited my right to be a fan. Thereafter my job would be to report who won and how. Nothing more.

Where Snead was involved this was difficult because I was undeniably a Snead fan. I loved to watch him swing the club. For 60 years I've been a Snead fan and friend and remain so today.

Throughout his long career Snead stirred up negative emotions of some who spoke unkindly of him. It never bothered Snead but it did me. Most of their disenchantment was from second hand rumors and misunderstandings to humor their own egos.

I've heard people tell how rude he was when pie-eyed in a bar in Phoenix. I knew Sam didn't drink, so that couldn't have been. Maybe a beer or wine at dinner but he was not a drinker. I had traveled too many miles with him not to know these stories were unfounded.

Sam had a reputation of burying his money in tomato cans in the backyard of his Hot Springs home. He may have encouraged the reputation of miserliness but he was neither stingy nor "cheap" in the sense of being a moocher.

When I hear that I tell this story.

A few months after I came home from WWII, not having seen any great golf or golfers for a couple of years, I contemplated going to Hot Springs and playing golf, possibly with him.

One night I phoned him, saying that Peggy, my wife, and I were thinking about coming down in three weeks and asked if he would be there that weekend and be able to play.

Snead said that sounded great. He would have to make a couple of phone calls but was sure it would be okay. He told me what train to catch. It stopped in Covington, VA, early in the morning and he'd be there to meet us.

"What about the phone calls," I asked, for I hadn't understood why he needed to call someone.

"I'll do that tomorrow," Sam said, "and I'll call you tomorrow night. I think I've got a couple of exhibitions that weekend and I need to call and cancel them until later."

That changed everything.

Exhibitions didn't pay as well in those days but he was going to get about $600 for Saturday and $1,000 for Sunday. If he cancelled out that $1,600 to play with us – no way.

I told him not to cancel until I was sure we could come. The next night I called and told him the trip was off, to go ahead with his exhibitions.

Don't get the idea Sam didn't like money. He

did, but sometimes other things had a value, too.

And sometimes getting a little money can be costly.

One year at the Tam O'Shanter tournament in Chicago, Snead shot 68 the first round and followed with a 66. I sat in the press room for his bubbling interview and then together we walked out toward the parking lot.

As we walked briskly, side by side, at about the same moment we both saw a dollar bill in the path ahead. Neither said a word but our pace quickened. When within a few feet, I dashed forward and planted my shoe on the bill.

Snead thought he could reach it quicker by grabbing for it and we got there simultaneously, him holding one end in his hand. The rest of it was under my foot.

"Lift up your foot," he said. "I saw it first."

"Yes, but I reached it first."

"Take your shoe off of I'll tear it in two."

No deal.

Sam reached in his pocket and gave me two quarters for my half. We each were 50 cents richer, but that 50 cents represented his entire winnings for the week.

In lunging to grab it first he had put his entire weight on his wrist and sprained it. Overnight it became swollen and sore.

When I arrived in the press room at Tam O'Shanter the next day there was a note on the bulletin board:

Sam had called in his withdrawal and none of the press ever had a chance to ask how he'd injured the wrist. I was sorry about the wrist but he was holding onto my dollar.

Snead was the most competitive athlete I ever knew. He lived with one goal – to win. I suspect there are many golfers today who would have more titles if they had the compulsion to be the best – as Snead and Nicklaus did. If it was tennis (and Sam was pretty good at it) or softball (and Sam once had to skip a month of the tour because he hurt his elbow, sliding into second in a caddie game) or playing cards, he was an aggressive competitor.

I recall a night at his home when, with our wives, we were playing bridge. I was not a very smart player and tended to underbid. Sam was the opposite. To the dismay of his partner he liked to bid. He seemed to bid if his cards were the same size, regardless of suit or value.

Near the end of a particularly disastrous bidding night Sam excused himself to go to the bathroom. Someone called to him to hurry back and this brought forth the old vaudeville joke... "Never mind, for the first time tonight I know what he has in his hand."

In 1957 a young Gary Player, who had followed the footsteps of Bobby Locke from South

Africa to America, was invited to the Greenbrier Festival pro-am.

On the last day Snead posted what looked like the winning score but word filtered back that Player was making a charge.

Snead's office in the pro shop overlooked the green of this par three, 18th hole. Sam had removed his spikes and slipped into his tasseled slippers. He turned to me and said, "That's an easy putt he has. If he makes it we are tied."

Player made it. Sam reached down, put on his spikes and called for his caddie. They headed for the range, some 150 yards away to loosen up. Sam had been in 40 minutes.

His practice bag was half empty when Player arrived for a little tune-up. Sam called for his caddie to come in, turned to Player and said... "Nice round. It looks like you and I have some more playing to do."

Off they went toward the first tee. The youngster had taken a 300-yard walk...but never hit a practice ball.

Cricket, before your mother and I could join the playoff gallery we had to relieve the babysitter, in whose care you had been all day. With a heavy seven-month-old spectator we arrived in time to see them halve at the first green.

They halved the second, then the third and then the fourth. Our bundle of spectator had become quite heavy and when they headed toward the fifth green, away from the club, we decided to stop walking, and if it went that far we'd rejoin them at the seventh.

Snead won the fifth, climbed in a golf cart and headed in. As he passed by I yelled to him, "You've taken so long I'm tired of holding the baby." Sam told his cart driver to stop. He came over, took you from me, and rode on toward the club.

We walked. When we got to the presentation stand, there you were, sitting in the 10-gallon sterling silver Revere Bowl, with Sam holding you in.

The first golf tournament you ever saw was won by Snead and for the award ceremony you had a front bowl seat.

Months earlier Sam had written you the first of two significant letters. This one, when you were barely a month old, he said in part... "I'd like to give you your first golf lesson. If you learn from either of your parents you'll be a hacker for life..."

The other letter from Snead to you detailed the victories he had scored while using that heavy duck canvas bag with his name on it, which he had given me when Wilson furnished him with a new leather bag. He removed the balls and tees first.

Keep that letter and the bag that was carried at the British Open (1946), PGA (1942) and the Masters (1949). The bag doesn't look like much, the shoulder strap is frayed from wear and it's not as bright as it once was, but on the side the stencil says Sam Snead. It was close to a lot of golf history. Three Grand Slam victories. Keep it.

There was a time when we almost came to blows. I got mad. Then Sam got mad. And Peggy thought she'd have to separate us.

I never won our friendly little matches and didn't expect to. Sam's give limit on strokes was six, three on each side. This usually meant four of the six were on par five holes, where I had no chance. Those were always birdie holes for him.

One day in Coral Gables I had been lucky and was only one down (with my strokes) on the back nine. After driving on No. 17, I had about a five-iron to the green. Sam was seldom a giver of advice unless it was a big money playing lesson. Before I played, and long before we would reach his drive, he suggested I was quitting at the bottom. "Go right on through. Finish high."

A practice swing and I followed his suggestion. The ball ended up about two feet from the cup. That birdie brought me even and the 18th (normally the 9th) was a par three. If I was ever to have a chance to win, this was it.

Up front, even, one to go. I checked everything – wind, distance, grip, height of the tee, swing-plane, position of the moon With No. 3 wood I would get it close, 195 yards away.

Wham. some calibration was wrong. The ball went straight up, up, up. Then down, down, down. It barely cleared the tee.

Sam had his four iron in hand. When he saw the wounded goose shot, he pounded the club on the ground, smiled that silly little grin of his and said, "You can tell what's in your neck."

He was laughing at me. I boiled.

I shouldn't have done it but I said... "...well, that may be so, but I never lost the National Open by taking eight on the last hole..."

Now he was muttering. The grin was gone.

"Let's not get nasty," he said as he whipped that iron like a dart to within four feet of the hole.

Peggy came back to call for sanity instead of insults. "Remember, boys, it's only a game."

Same old result, one down each nine. I never did win.

That was truly one of the golden eras of golf when, week after week, you could watch Snead, Hogan, Nelson, Demaret and the like.

The next golden era was Palmer, Player and Nicklaus and I was fortunate enough to see them grow up to be golf's royalty. Each had such a different personality, but all great players.

Hagen, Jones and Sarazen were just about past their prime when I began reporting golf. Their skills may have diminished but their charisma was still brilliant even if I didn't know what to call it. I never played with Hagen but watched him and that trio hold forth until the next and the next and the next.

There will be other superstars. Golf creates its galaxy and they, too, will thrill others who love golf as I do.

It was the first and only annual convention of the National Boxing Association I ever attended and I went to it largely because it was in nearby Winston-Salem, 30 miles from home.

At that time the NBA was the one and only organization supervising the sport/business of boxing in the USA. As such it attracted all of the major promoters, managers, fighters and hangers-on, of which there were a sizable number even in those pre-television days.

Everyone was expected to check in at the registration desk, pay a modest fee and receive your dinner ticket and name-tag. I joined the line and moved up to the desk. Then to the ballroom where the pre-dinner dance had begun.

Having been born with "two left feet" I did not cut a particular graceful figure on the dance floor and was much more at ease watching and envying those who could...

Winston-Salem's finest were supporting this national event that had come to their city. All were hospitable, anxious to make it a success.

Several people attracted my attention as they looked at me in that way that lets you know they are trying to recall your name or your face or are commenting on your wild tie. I continued to move around the room, doing my own star-gazing at the big names of boxing, hoping to find material for a column.

About then an attractive matron, sensing my solitude strolling, asked if I'd like to dance. As she did I glanced at her name tag and noticed she was a Reynolds. If your name is Reynolds in Winston-Salem chances were you are important.

The music was good. The lady was graceful and I managed not to step on her shoes as we did several turns. Then intermission, my favorite time.

"I've never seen you fight," she said, "but my husband tells me you are the greatest."

Stop. Hold it, my mind said. Something's wrong.

"I beg your pardon," I said. "I am not a boxer. Your husband must have mistaken me for someone else."

She pointed to my name tag and asked, "Aren't you Jack Dempsey?"

"Heavens no. I'm John Derr from Greensboro. They must have mixed up the name tags. Dempsey was checking in at the same time and the lady reached over to the names that started with 'D' arranged in alphabetical order, with DEmpsey next to DErr."

Man, was I glad she wanted to dance instead of fight.

Years later when I would visit his restaurant Jack would occasionally ask, jokingly... "Are you still wearing my name tag?"

Let's look back to the decade of the 20's and the great sports stars who performed during that time: Jack Dempsey, Bobby Jones, Babe Ruth and Harold (Red) Grange. Probably less known than the other three, Grange excelled equally or maybe better in his sport than the other stars did in theirs. A Mount Rushmore tableau would have featured all four. It was my pleasure to know them all, but if you wanted a football hero – it was Harold (Red) Grange.

Born in 1903, Grange was forced by an old injury to quit playing the game in 1934 but in the first third of the last century the football exploits of the "Galloping Ghost " were almost unbelievable. He was Harry Potter before there was a Harry Potter. After a highly successful high school career, the lad from Wheaton enrolled at the University of Illinois. When he learned that more than 100 players were trying out for the football team, he wondered if all his high school records at Wheaton would be worth anything at Illinois. Late in his freshman year Grange carried the ball one time. Only one. Result -- one touchdown.

They knew who he was when another season began. Now for some real play. The season was going well. The Illini had a brand new Memorial Stadium, named as a tribute to the WWI veterans. October 18, 1924 was to be Dedication Day. A crisp day in the Mid West, it was perfect for a football game against your favorite foe.

Illinois was playing undefeated Michigan, an arch Big Ten rival. Kickoff time finally. Boom. A young 175 pound sophomore, wearing uniform No. 77, clutched the bounding ball on his five-yard stripe and headed East. Red Grange ran 95 yards, zigged a little, zagged a little, sped by the last foe and scored. Many of the 66,000 fans had not even found their seats. 95 yards, cheers.

Minutes later, second time with the ball, Illinois was at its own 33 yard line. One play later that kid wearing No. 77 again clutched the ball and headed East...67 yards, his second touchdown. This one shorter. A few minutes later Grange needed to run only 56 yards to score. He seemed to enjoy it and before the first quarter had reached the 12 minute mark the " Galloping Ghost" ran another 44 yards and scored. In the first 12 minutes of this anticipated close match, Red Grange scored four touchdowns and Illinois led. 27-0.

There was more. A shorty of 11 yards

was his No. 5, but then he threw a 20-yard scoring heave, making his contribution now six touchdowns. (One wonders if Coach Bob Zuppke had not heard the Wolverines crying 'uncle.') The final score was 39-14, with Grange figuring in every score. What an afternoon! What a halfback!

Three times an All-American, Grange's college career saw him run 3,362 yards, score 31 touchdowns and complete 40 of 82 passes for 575 yards. On the day after his last college game, Grange was persuaded by owner Coach George Halas to turn professional and sign a pro contract with the Chicago Bears. The tandem, Halas and Grange, enjoyed much success, barnstorming their way across America, drawing applauding crowds. Their success helped put the NFL on firmer footing. That combo may even have saved it.

It's been reported that when the pair visited the White House and were introduced to President Calvin Coolidge, as Coach George Halas and Red Grange of the Chicago Bears, it drew a pleasant smile and this remark from the President: "That's nice. I have always enjoyed the animal acts."

That little tidbit was not known by me in 1952 when I could have asked Grange if it was true. That spring I spent almost two weeks with Grange and West Point's Glenn Davis making a movie, a two-reeler, in Chicago. It was a situation football story in which Grange would propose a play, Davis would try to execute it and I would pass judgment. I wore a stupid striped shirt and was billed as the Referee, which oddly enough was the name of the movie. But you know these movie folks.

Yes, I know you never heard of it. Not many people did.

But it was a delightful experience with these two great halfbacks, both All-Americans in different years, different eras. Each was rated very highly, all-time greats, by the football experts.

One lunch time, we talked about the injuries that forced both Grange and Davis from the pro game and the oddity that in their very early years each had overcome threatening health problems, only to later tear up the gridirons in the rough game of football.

Davis hurt his knee playing sandlot football in California. It was an injury that eventually would end his playing career after West Point and his Army service. Red's restriction came after an illness when he was six or seven, he told Davis and me one day. His family doctor explained to his father, the

Wheaton police chief, that young Harold, who was being treated for a cold also had an active heart murmur. That was a surprise. The doctor decreed that Harold should be withheld from all sports and strenuous exercise.

Not a good message for an active sub-teenager, but little Harold, whose mother had died when he was five, sneaked out and played with friends, as long and as rough as he wanted. Kids will do that. He told no one at school he was benched, so he played every sport. Six years later a new doctor told him and his dad, the earlier report was not correct. It was a wrong diagnosis.

But Daddy didn't know that Harold had never slowed down, not then, nor when he drove a truck, delivering ice to homes and stores in Wheaton. Already a high school standout, Grange used this summer job, hauling heavy slabs of ice to pay his tuition. Thus another nickname was born.... "the Wheaton Ice Man." This was a suitable companion to the popular "Galloping Ghost."

Davis said his early knee injury stayed with him. He would have it wrapped tightly during play and practice. When he completed his military service, he joined the pros back in California. It's not a child's sport, Davis agreed without complaining, but he suffered an unusually strong hit, and that ended his career with the LA Rams. He worked for years in promotion for the Los Angeles Times, succumbed to cancer at the age of 80 in 2005. He was Army's "Mr. Inside" teamed with Doc Blanchard, "Mr. Outside." These All America backs were a pair without peers in Army's good days. I relished these off-hours in Chicago with Davis and Grange.

While chinning with these two stars one day I felt a twinge in my long-ago healed right knee – the one that sometimes bent backward when I was about their disabling age. I thought better than to mention to them that my right knee had a mind of its own. It now seemed minor. They'd have played right through it.

Grange stayed around football throughout his life. In addition to our time in Chicago on the movie lot, Red and I broadcast several games, including the Senior Bowl in Mobile, where he did the color commentary.

Today we can rate our athletes as we see them on television. In Grange's day, television was barely in its infancy and we learned of the exploits of our heroes through radio announcers such as Ted Husing, Graham McNamee and Bill Stern. We saw through their eyes, not always without favorites. The grainy old movies of that era were fine, we thought, but it would have been wonderful to see "the greatest halfback in all American football" dashing toward the end zone. What a Galloping Ghost he was.

Grange died at his home in Florida at 87.

That decade of the 1920's certainly had the stars and I was fortunate enough to have worked with Grange, played with Jones on his home course, survived two mixed up convention name tags with Dempsey, who was wearing mine. Ruth, the other member of my athletic Mount Rushmore, passed away without me seeing him play, but I was honored to do his obituary tribute on Edward R. Murrow's CBS radio program when I was in Paris after the 1948 Olympics. Ruth had been a frequent guest on Red Barber's CBS radio show and during the wait before airtime, I was privileged to talk with Ruth until it was time to escort him into Barber's studio. Those were memorable times.

Yes, the 20's were an exciting time, even if only to recall.

E. Harvie Ward, who was later to win many titles, among them the USGA Amateur and British Amateur, was a slightly-built 15-year-old phenom when he grabbed his first significant trophy.

Ward had run out of competition in eastern North Carolina. His hometown of Tarboro did not even have a course of its own so he was always "on the road." This may have helped his game, becoming familiar with so many different type courses.

His druggist father let Harvie enter the North Carolina Junior Championship, which had been the springboard for many outstanding young golfers. It was played at Sedgefield CC.

Harvie was assigned a caddie, one of the Sedgefield staff, who stood about 6'2". Even wearing his new spiked shoes, a novelty for him, Harvie was no more than 5'2," if that. They made quite a contrast walking down the fairway.

Through three rounds of match play no opponent bothered young Ward too much but the new shoes did. He persevered.

In the finals, with Harvie only one up at the turn, he began to be really unhappy with those shoes.

I was walking with his father and there were maybe 75 folks in the gallery for the diminutive lad had become a favorite. Going down the dog-leg 13th fairway, still only one up, Harvie drifted back to speak to his father.

He asked if he may get out of those shoes and play barefoot. His dad approved and off came the spikes. He handed them to the tall caddie who tied the laces together and slung them over the bag. They moved ahead.

Shoeless, Harvie closed out the match, 3 and 2, and his first big title was won by the barefoot warrior.

There had been another shoeless champion three years before in the 1938 Canadian Open. Sam Snead married his childhood sweetheart, Audrey, and they went north on a golfing honeymoon.

On the last nine of the 36 holes played on the final day, Snead felt blisters forming on his heels. He took off his shoes and played the last seven holes bare-footed, no shoes, no socks.

When Prime Minister Massey, a brother of Raymond Massey, the actor, was presenting Sam the golden Seagram trophy, he remarked that Snead's 277 had not broken the tournament record but that he would be recognized as the first player ever to win the Canadian Open... in his bare feet.

Snead, never at a loss for words, sent the gallery into a roar when he turned to the Prime Minister and said:

"Mr. Prime Minister, I'm up here on my honeymoon. You don't need shoes on a honeymoon."

Popularly known by America's golfing public as 'Champagne Tony,' young Mr. Anthony David Lema began to make his mark on the PGA golf tour in 1955, after having served as an active Marine in the Korean War. That was not a breeding ground for shy but when Tony could lay down his rifle and pick up his driver there was no more shyness in this young Californian.

Lema learned when he was just a youngster, living in Oakland with his widowed mother and three siblings, if you wanted to eat you had to get to the table early. His father died when Tony was three years old. Tony hunted odd jobs to do what he could to help his mother but had neither the interest nor the opportunity to play golf. After Korea with no job in sight, he applied for and received a starting job at a San Francisco golf club. Being exposed to the game and learning he was pretty good at it, he didn't waste the opportunity to improve. In two years Lema was good enough to play, but not good enough to win. He broke loose in 1962.

In October of that year he began a great streak of championship golf. In the next four years he won 12 official PGA Tour events. He was second on 11 occasions and third four times.

You know, when you're young and eager, sometimes you make promises .... what you want to do, what you expect to do and sometimes you do. In October of 1962 Tony remarked to those who would listen that he expected to win the Orange County open, being played at Costa Mesa, CA. "And when I win," he told Nelson Cullenward and the other California writers, "I will serve champagne to you gentlemen of the press." He did. Thus was born his chummy moniker, "Champagne Tony."

How did he win and toast the happy press? He beat Bob Rosburg in a playoff. You remember Rossie? A pretty good win.

Tony was moved up in class. Second by one stroke to Jack Nicklaus at the 1963 Masters, he was also a major threat at the Open that year. He miscalculated as others had done before him. Tony thought he needed birdies on the last two holes to get a tie at the Open. He bogeyed each, finished two shots back.

But he won --at Mobile, at Memphis, the Bing Crosby and the rich Thunderbird. Our television network picked him up at the Cleveland open, on the Highland Park course. This was late in June 1964. Two items are recalled involving Tony at that event, the last he played before winning the British Open, two weeks later, besting Nicklaus by five strokes at Saint Andrews.

Lema is remembered for two incidents at Cleveland that week. Some years before I had devised a scoring pattern, which I filled out after each day's play. The last 18 players would be listed, showing their hole-by-hole score. Having plotted the course, noting easier holes and tougher holes, told me who had played which holes better and, importantly, who had done worse on the tough ones. This would let me predict, before Saturday, who would win. It even amazed me with its accurate mathematical prediction.

Several of the players knew I played around with my unique scorekeeping. They would ask, in a friendly manner, if they had a chance to win. Once I recall have encountered Palmer far out on the course one Sunday morning as I checking my yardages at an unfamiliar layout.

"What are my chances, John? Let me see your note book." I withheld it but he insisted. I said: "You are not even in the book." Just tell it like it is. Sure enough he didn't win.

On Sunday mornings we used to tape 3 to 5 minutes of players in mini interviews, put the tape on hold. The director could insert these fillers later while players were walking between shots. I never thought much could be learned watching men walking.

At Cleveland this Sunday I noticed Lema had scored a bogey on the 5th hole-- all three days. This was his only hole with as many as two bogeys. Tony was idling by the putting green when I asked him to record a short tape. I began by noting he was only two behind and seemed in shape to win again. Okay. When I asked him what was his trouble on the 5th, a rather ordinary par 4, he bristled.

"No, John. I will not discuss that hole. Three times I bogeyed it, yes. I don't want to talk about a hole I played poorly. Now find a hole with three birdies, we can talk. I put bogies out of my mind." I understood. No interview today, just watch the walkers.

Now we near the finish. Palmer is ahead but Lema is rolling. A cluster of birdies moves him up. Palmer had the big crowd, as usual. He was popular in Cleveland where he had spent some military duty, but Champagne Tony had his own followers and the appreciative spectators were enjoying the battle. Tony finished with a 65 at 270. Arnie's birdie effort failed and they tied after 72 holes.
A tie, the bane of most non-fans involved in golf tournaments.

This was a quirky coverage deal where the TV network was committed to produce a Sunday winner, sudden death if needed. No next day action disrupts schedules like another 18 holes.

Problem No. 1. The playoff would start on the first hole. No cameras. No phone lines. Somebody in operations had goofed, big time, agreeing with the sponsors and tour to let it start on No. 1.

Our HSN director, a bushy haired buddy from Brooklyn, accustomed to emergencies, had a solution. With foresight he had gone to the club officials and asked if they could provide a couple of low power shortwave radios in case we needed them. They did. Where they found them, I never knew, but we had radios.

Ray Scott, the celebrated voice of the Green Bay Packers, was our anchor. Working blind, 500 yards from the action where the playoff would begin. Scott was given one radio. He stayed on the tower with his outgoing TV microphone. Incidentally, Scott was absolutely tops in his announcing of golf or any sport and I was glad he was on board.

The other radio was given to me, with instructions to go to the first tee, set the stage and describe the tee shots of Palmer and Champagne Tony. With no cameras, their shots would be seen -not by millions- but the few hundred who could eyeball them with me.

It was a very unusual TV playoff --no camera, no mikes, no spotters. I stood aside and radioed to Scott as they teed off. Both players missed the fairway, Lema left, Palmer right. With his capable ability to set a scene, even with no picture for anyone to see, Scott told our audience what they might hear but could not see as the playoff between the popular friends got underway.

Meanwhile, relying on memory and minimal observation, I pictured, in words, the second shots each would have in going for the green. Speaking softly, a habit not necessary here, the players being 250 yards away, I walked and talked into the ancient radio.

Scott asked me to move away from the crowd, some voices were overriding my reports. I did, climbing the hill. The actual green was not in my vision. Over the radio I heard "are they on the green?" I explained I still could not see. Again I was asked, more intently, "where on the green?" Listeners must have heard our exchanges and wondered, are they both blind?

SCOTT: "I am stuck here on the tower. I need help. Are they on the green yet and how far?"

He paused, then pleaded with me to answer. Again we both heard noises on our radio line. I had to guess at his question, but I knew what he'd ask or so I thought.

DERR: "No, not yet. Palmer is playing now. He's played. His approach should be on the green somewhere. I don't know. Now here's Lema. He's clearly on the green, and much closer than Arnie. I am now up to the edge of the green. I can see."

VOICE: Where did you say you are on green?

DERR: "Palmer's ball is 25-30 feet away. Lema is much closer, maybe about seven or eight."

VOICE: "Where?"

DERR: "Like I said he's much closer, maybe 7 feet. The way he putted on the back nine this match might soon be over."

SCOTT: "The crowd sounds like Palmer

missed."

DERR: "Yes his putt slipped by, it trembled but didn't drop."

SCOTT: "Move back some. I'm still getting noisy break up from your mike. Are you holding it too close?"

DERR: "Same as you, but Lema just made his birdie so that will be all from here. They are walking back up the hill and I will be there soon. Ray, we should never try this again with only radios. I think these were military surplus from 1918."

As I made it back to the clubhouse, the fans who had heard Scott's part of this most unusual broadcast were openly amused about something. It beat me. They seemed to have gotten a kick, hearing a radio telecast with no cameras. Scott tumbled down from his tower to explain. And when I heard the story, I laughed, too.

It seems the club officials who scrounged up two shortwave radios had not known they were both set on the wave length frequency used by a Cleveland taxicab company. A cab driver was sent to pick up a passenger, out by the golf course. He was unaware he was in the middle of a national broadcast, just trying to find his passenger, waiting somewhere for him on Green street.

All he knew was he couldn't find his passenger. Where, oh, where? Neither Ray nor

I had known that the street behind the first hole was GREEN Street. The cabbie, our fellow broadcaster, had his problem... we had ours. On Green, but where?

There could have been more than the Cleveland Open at stake that day. Lema's next outing was the Open at Saint Andrews, where he used Arnie's old caddie, Tip Anderson, and a Palmer putter to win the Claret Jug. Win it he did, beating Jack Nicklaus by five strokes. Do you think the putter and ol' Tip helped him win?

In another memory of Lema, the pride of Portugal, I recall him at a Sponsor/Press day. Tony had won the Thunderbird Classic the year before and this day of playing with Lema was a perk for the sponsoring Ford Dealers in the Met NY area. It was played at the Upper Montclair CC, where I was a member.

Lema was to play three holes with trios of Ford dealers. He would play three holes, then join the next group of dealers and drop back and forth. Eventually it came time for my group to acquire Lema on the fourth tee. Tony was introduced to the Ford dealers. We left the tee, with everybody walking, no carts. I knew Tony was shy, but it was uncomfortable when he insisted on talking and walking with me. I said "Tony I'd like to talk with you but really you should be talking with the Ford people, because they're the ones that are putting up the purse money."

"But I don't know them," Tony said. "Well, they know you," I said, "and it would help for you

to talk with them, not me."
Nevertheless, the Ford dealers were enjoying being with Tony.

I had a good time at my three holes... three pars. Tony bogeyed the second of our three, so this gave me a conversation piece for the rest of the summer. It let me brag "I beat Tony Lema, by one hole, the last time we played." And that was the last time. And it was true.

Tony left us much too soon. The day after the 1966 PGA championship, Tony, 32, and his wife, Betty, 30, were in a chartered plane leaving the Firestone club to play an exhibition in Illinois. The plane ran out of gas and crashed on a golf course. Tony and his charming wife were both killed and it was the end of a great, great golfer, great friend. I don't know how great his greatness would have been, but in a very short time he had made a tremendous impression on everybody.

In a forest of tall trees, Tony Lema stood high.

For two fortnights the converted luxury liner, USS West Point, would be home base for the 80th Fighter Group, including my 89th Fighter Squadron and several thousand others on an overseas military mission – destination uncertain.

The gentle breezes of rumors that sprung up when orders to pack barracks bags and gas masks had officially been posted had now escalated. Some ex-Boy Scouts had prepared themselves with maps of Europe, North Africa, the Mediterranean and the Far East. There were no maps of India seen.

Instead of subsiding, once we had steamed out of New York harbor shortly after a very dark midnight, the rumor winds had reached tornadic levels. For some of us it was easier to adopt a fatalistic point of view. We were enroute to somewhere and this was not the Staten Island ferry.

Daylight revealed a not too distant coastline to the starboard side. See, not even 12 hours at sea, we'd learned the nautical terms for right and left. Some who recognized land sights on shore assured the rest of us we were off the Jersey coast, heading south with land in view.

Since daybreak several Navy patrol planes had been visible, trailing our wake and then angling off to right or left but always returning to follow behind us. This gave credence to the rumor that they were assigned to protect us and drop depth charges on any German submarines that may have been lying in wait.

It seemed to be another logical rumor but one with no verification. If a rumor can't be proved or disproved there's almost no length to which one's inventiveness can go. A rumor, if proven, becomes a fact and is no longer a rumor.

Some time about 11 o'clock on our second day at sea, our attention was called to more escort planes. We must have been near the Virginia coast or maybe Cape Hatteras by then.

At first there seemed to be only a single plane trailing us, but while we looked three more came into view. These came closer than the ones the day before.

While the lead plane descended nearer the water, maybe 1000 or 1500 feet above, the other three were in a triangle formation behind and above it.

I didn't see it. I don't think I saw anything but others crowded along the rail of the aft deck on unofficial watch yelled, "Something fell out of that plane. I saw it."

More overactive imagination, I thought.

And then we all saw. A geyser of water rose abruptly out of the Atlantic. Up quick. Down quick. Over?

Not quite. In seconds an object surfaced

above the level of the waves. Probably a half-mile or more behind us. We had not yet learned to judge distances at sea but this object was clearly visible but only for a few seconds. It appeared to be of a metallic darkish color with no recognizable shape. Some thought it was conical, others said it looked like a box.

We never knew. The Germans did report, erroneously, their subs had pursued and sunk the USS West Point, identifying it by name in their communiqué. We figured maybe the Nazi news had been garbled. Some pilot might have said, as others did during the war, "Sighted sub. Sank same."

Rio de Janiero was our first port of call. Refueled and headed across the South Atlantic, a bigger body of water than we had ever imagined, and one day blended endlessly into another.

In the North Atlantic, even in wartime, one could see other ships in the sea lanes, sometimes traveling in convoys. In the South Atlantic there were no other ships and because the speedy USS West Point was without escort it seemed more lonely.

Moonlight nights were welcomed. The uneven cresting of the waves, rippling white caps creating their own unique patterns in the moonlight served to break the monotony of water, water.

There was another diversion of sorts but I've always suspected it was more a ploy to dispel boredom of the troops than a significant contribution to the war effort.

Periodically various elements drew the assignment of "submarine lookout watch." Several hundred men were stationed around the perimeter of the USS West Point with instructions to swivel our heads, rotate our eyes and "look for subs or other foreign objects." in the water.

Our squadron took the assignment seriously and on our four-hour watch we swiveled our heads and watched – but never saw so much as a flying fish, much less a German submarine. If I had thought this was our only protection from attack by a sub, I really would have worried.

Lookouts were not needed when land was sighted again. The news burst forth from a thousand throats. High above the buildings of a town we saw in the distance loomed Table Mountain, familiar from school geography books as a landmark of Capetown, South Africa. Just as the Christ of the Andes monument had told us we were near Rio, Table Mountain did the same for us here.

Shore leave was given here and a visit to the local USO afforded the opportunity to meet a friendly local family. The next day they drove us up the mountain for a picnic lunch. Later we visited several churches and saw many original Rembrandt paintings that had been sent there for safe keeping.

Capetown was an interesting, friendly

town. Not too many Americans had stopped there. Mostly their service visitors had been from Australia or England. It seemed far removed from the shooting war, but a day later we learned that was not the case.

The swift USS West Point eased out of Capetown after midnight, silently resuming our voyage. The night before we were instructed to rustle around in our barracks bags and change to woolen uniforms. This seemed odd, since obviously we were now headed for the warmer Indian ocean.

Not so.

When we left Capetown harbor, instead of going East around the Cape of Good Hope, we were headed straight South toward Antarctica and the South Pole.

This time the rumor was confirmed. A pack of Nazi subs had assembled at the tip of Africa to lie in wait on the course they expected the USS West Point to take. By changing directions, we had foiled their plan...and felt some polar breezes, too.

After two days in the cold, blustery weather the Captain headed East and North but this evasion meant we would need to refuel sooner than planned.

As we neared land again, maps were studied and the more knowledgeable G.I.s deduced we were headed into the harbor of Diego Suarez near the northern tip of Madagascar. Capetown and Rio we knew about but all we knew of this port was that the Germans had penetrated the harbor defense a few weeks earlier and sunk many ships of the French fleet.

Half-sunken hulls were painfully visible in the harbor and the captain had to slowly pick his way through the wrecked remains to get to a refueling station. We could not dock there. One wondered where had these subs gone...or had they?

Again underway the weather turned warm. Many of us left the crowded hammock area, brought blankets above and slept on deck, unmindful of the nearly nightly showers that came.

Warm breezes became hot breezes as we neared India.

When we docked in the busy port of Calcutta, we thought that was the end of our nautical odyssey. Not so.

The First Sergeant of our outfit was a nosey old veteran. He learned the 80th Fighter Group would be transferred to a smaller coastal vessel for our final leg to Karachi, on the other coast of India.

Units scheduled for transfer assembled at a lower gang plank and with bag and baggage made what seemed a perilous passage across a foot bridge from our ship to a harbor barge and then across the bay to our new ship.

Above us floated several dozen sausage-shaped balloons, aloft to serve as a harbor defense should Japanese planes venture this far into India. This was our first actual sight of defense emplacements and brought a new view of potential danger for our Stateside troops.

Locally-based soldiers calmed our anxiety when they reported the balloons were mostly a morale-building ploy for local consumption. Their questionable value as a deterrent to air attacks had never been tested. Relax.

The transfer was completed about noon. Three hours later the air raid sirens wailed from every corner of the huge city. Three Japanese planes, high above the balloons, dropped bombs that fell harmlessly in the water. That lone raid was the only – only – time any bombs fell on Calcutta during the war.

I heard the sirens but did not see either the planes or the bombs and let me tell you why.

That same day wily veteran First Sergeant had learned our new ship would have four plush staterooms. He told a few of us that as soon as we were aboard we should quickly search out these rooms, go in with our bags and promptly undress to our underwear.

Tom Armistead and I, along with two sergeants, found a room and did as we were told. Here were beds, beds with white sheets on them, pillows, fans and a bathroom. All the comforts of home – comforts we had not seen for 27 days.

Sleeping quarters were not assigned on this

leg of the voyage and a steady stream of people cracked open the door, looking for a choice place to bunk. There were privates and sergeants. There were captains and lieutenants.

As soon as the door opened, one of us, usually the First Sergeant, boomed out... "What do you want, soldier?"

It was that last word – soldier – that preserved our privacy. It usually brought an apologetic, muffled reply as the door quietly closed. Even the officers backed out without questioning the authoritative demeaning words.

Confirmed theory: A body clothed only in boxer shorts isn't much different whether it be a General or a Private.

Our renegade foursome left one man – in his underwear – on guard duty at all times, and for two days and nights, on the trip around the tip of India, en route to Karachi, we slept and luxuriated like Eastern potentates in "our" stateroom.

A trip that began with concave, sagging hammocks deep in the bowels of USS West Point, ended in real beds with sheets.

In the military they tell you...Rank Has Its Privileges. R.H.I.P. is certainly a truism as every dogface knows. But let it be known... "A nearly naked man has his own rank."

For us R.H.I.P. was "Rest Here In Privacy."

It is not in Tibet. Instead, the Balsams Grand Resort Hotel is in an uppermost corner of New Hampshire's White Mountains, 13 miles from Canada. If there is a Shangri La in America it is at Dixville Notch, N.H., and that's why you might expect to see Ronald Colman walking through the luxuriant lobby.

You may not have heard of the Balsams but it's not one of these glitzy new glass and aluminum creations. The Balsams has been serving guests since 1866. Since that first building with 25 guests rooms, much has been added. Today there are 232 guest rooms, surrounded by 15,000 acres of private unspoiled nature preserve. And two golf courses.

In 1912 one guest who signed the register came there at work – not on vacation. His name was Donald Ross. He put his signature on the hotel register but, more importantly, he put his signature on a marvelous 18-hole golf course that, with teams of oxen, he carved out of and around the western side of Keyser mountain.

Unlike some of the hundreds of courses designed by Ross, the Panorama, as this scenic layout is known, commanded his personal attention. Ross was not only concerned with routing the holes, but he had to design and supervise the construction of the primitive equipment needed to move unwanted granite from the rolling fairways and bordering rough.

There are still outcroppings of granite but they stand visible and one need not worry about breaking a hand or a club on a stone Ross failed to extricate. History records that Dixville Notch, as many other parts of North America, was at one time beneath the sea. The rocks are only remnants of a layer that was approximately 20,000 feet thick. It's no wonder that Ross found some that even his oxen could not budge.

The Panorama, old as it is, was not the first course here. Charles Thom built a six-hole course for hotel guests in 1897. It was abandoned when Ross moved around the mountain to lay out today's course, flattening the tallest peak for the clubhouse. From it through the notches and over the lower peaks of the White Mountains one can see Quebec, Vermont and almost Maine, only 15 miles away but behind a higher peak.

The Panorama has been lengthened in recent decades. The blue tees, from which it measures 6,804 yards with a slope rating of 136, have been extended backward. On many of the holes the red or forward tees occupy the same area where Ross placed his regular tees.

From the red tees it plays 5,069 yards with a 124 slope rating. Only the expert players tackle the Panorama from the blues. The more accommodating white or club tees provide a 6,100 yard course, rated at 130.

The greens have been retained with the

trademark of the revered architect. By current standards they may be considered small. Almost all are crowned and slope to all four sides. Ross was cognizant of the need for quick drainage after snow and rain and throughout the course one can see how, even in 1912, he built his greens with that in mind.

One other characteristic of the greens is the influence the location of Keyser mountain has on the way they break. This is true on most mountain courses, a la the Palm Springs question of "which way is Indigo?"

Bunkering is minimal and usually to the right or left of the green to serve directionally rather than punitively. For the most part the bunkers have a level floor, very good sand, and the sides are grassed, another Ross trademark.

Being 2,220 feet above sea level may add a few yards carry to a well-struck shot, but no one complains. One upslope par three, listed at 175 yards, plays more like 200.

After five holes of rolling terrain, almost meadow like, take a deep breath on the 18th tee. This par five is 560 uphill yards long. The elevation rises 145 feet from the tee box to the green. Visible beyond the green sits the old clubhouse, a welcome sight with its promise of libation and sustenance, a reward for having challenged Mr. Ross at his best.

Add up your score but don't dwell on it. You will know you have experienced a great day on one of America's most scenic courses. Absorbing the view may have affected your play. Lakes, ponds, meadows and mountains have captured your attention and you well might have seen a 1,600-pound moose munching in the wetlands. Moose are plentiful in this northern range.

The Balsams, known as the "Switzerland of America" is much more than a 1912 Donald Ross golf course. In fact, many of the guests who occupy its 232 rooms, winter and summer, never play the course or the shorter nine hole track by the hotel.

They come for the scenery and the world-class cuisine, which has earned top-awards recognition. Their menu reads like a phone book. The luncheon buffet table is 100 feet long. The dining room can seat 500 guests and with local staff exceeding 400 persons, service is prompt and pleasant.

This Grand Resort Hotel, self-sufficient even to the extent of generating its own heat and electricity, utilizes the true American plan. For guests there are no extra charges, except your golf cart and film for your minicam. You'll take a lot of pictures, regardless of ski season or golf season. They can serve to whet your appetite for your next visit. You will come back. The Balsams has 83% of its guests return on a regular basis.

It's not Tibet, but Tibet has no Donald Ross course.

ABOVE THE NOISE

Prior to the new fall broadcast season CBS Radio used to host a party in a New York hotel, bringing together their top entertainers from Hollywood, their most valued commercial sponsors, their advertising agencies and the press. If a promotional party could be identified as a gala this was one.

In September, 1953, I was invited to attend. This episode shows how an overheard conversation can have gigantic and unexpected results.

Jack Benny was a top star for CBS and the crowded room was standing with William Paley, founder and president of the network. A friend introduced me to an agency man while we were standing close to Paley and Benny, a couple of feet away.

As usual at gatherings of this type, if you want to be heard you sometimes have to almost shout. In making the introduction my friend spoke loudly.

There must have been one of those absolutely silent moments that sometimes occur in a noisy room at the moment he was introducing me. Above the noise my name filtered through.

Benny, whom I had never met, turned to me and asked "Did he say John Derr?" Nodding affirmatively, I held out my hand.

"I'm glad to meet you," Benny said. "That was a great series of shows you did from Carnoustie. All of us were rooting for Hogan to come through. I left the studio early every day so I could be able to listen at home. That must have been a great experience."

To a young country boy from North Carolina who had spent many youthful hours laughing at the comedy antics of Jack Benny, this was pretty heady stuff. Of course I realized he was anxious to know how his friend, Hogan, was doing, but the fact that he'd gone home to hear my reports was exhilarating.

I had been in Mr. Paley's presence a number of times but I realized he didn't know me from Adam. When Benny went on to ask more questions about the British Open there was body movement from Mr. Paley, implying that he had heard and liked them, too.

That might have ended the episode except Bing Crosby, whom I had met, ambled by and joined in the conversation about Hogan.

Crosby hosted the PGA pro-am at Pebble Beach and although NBC, ABC and Mutual had tried, no network ever came up with a sponsor. This was a sore spot with Bing. Here he was, putting on an outstanding charity tournament with the very top Hollywood celebrities and pro golfers and the networks couldn't sell it.

With an ally like Benny in hand, Crosby turned to Mr. Paley and said he wanted CBS to do the radio coverage on his event next January and he wanted it sponsored.

Even though no sponsor was in sight, Mr. Paley agreed that CBS Radio would broadcast it. If you own the network you can do that. Crosby had one other request. He asked that I be sent to California to do the play-by-play. I heard no commitment.

When time neared to put it on our schedule, to order phones lines and engineering, a month before the tournament, it was still not sold. No takers, even with Bing helping out. On all sustaining (unsold) shows for purposes of economy we used local announcers.

I set up the program to be staffed entirely by West Coast personnel with minimal travel costs.

Crosby found that out and called Mr. Paley, asking why I was not flying out to share the microphone with him. Next day I got orders to head for Pebble Beach.

It was lucky Bing had a big home right on the course. He asked me to stay there. He had other house guests, including Dolores and Bob Hope and a starlet friend.

The night before the tournament, in those days, there was a grand Calcutta. Already such betting ventures were frowned on by the USGA and Crosby took no part in it except to open the program and welcome his guests. As he and Bob prepared to drive over to the Inn, Bing told me they would be gone only a few minutes and I didn't need to go unless I wanted to.

Hope, in his inimitable humor, said, "Damned if that's so. He's going with us. I'm not leaving him here with Dolores."

The broadcasts were not sold but we shared the mike and had a lot of fun reporting, especially the travails of Bing's Hollywood friends. Bing was a funny man, on or off the air.

An example of the kind of person Crosby was, at least in his time with me. We were walking down a street near the Inn and a tall gentleman was on the other side of the road walking in our direction.

"Do you know who that is?" Bing asked. I said I didn't. "That's Johnny Mack Brown." Then I knew who he was. A former Alabama football player, Brown was a great Western star, truly a matinee idol.

Instead of crossing over to meet Brown, Crosby called to him, "Come over here, Mack, I want you to meet a friend of mine." Most folks would have done it the other way.

Crosby was a thoughtful person. One day at Pebble I said I had toured Chinatown looking for unusual frogs for Peggy's frogatorium. I explained that her collection of some 350 frogs included glass, wooden, porcelain and almost every other material as our friends from around the world added to her collection.

He asked if she had any brass frogs. Told

that she had solid brass likenesses, he said he would get her one made unlike any in her collection. He knew a craftsman in Monterey who used plumbing materials to create knick-knacks. A few days later he sent her a custom-made frog, really a "one-of-a-kind." Bing had gone to the man's shop and explained how he wanted it made.

Until his death after a golf game in Spain we remained in touch. A month before he died, he wrote me a three-paged letter describing the problems he was having with the PGA in running his charity tournament, trying to meet their requirements. He was not happy.

Several times he came to the Masters and strolled the course like any other golf fan. On one of his last visits there an amusing episode happened.

It was late in the day of the second round and I had joined the gallery at the 18th. Play was almost finished and as I strode toward the clubhouse I chanced to run into my sister, Eleanor, who lived in Atlanta. I had been unable to get her tickets and was surprised to see her in the throng at the Masters.

"Gee, I wish I had known you were here," I told her. "There are some people here I would have liked to introduce to you."

As we chatted I spotted Crosby walking up the hill toward the clubhouse. I broke in to tell her... "There goes Crosby, for instance...."

"Oh, I've met him already."

How did that happen, I asked.

"You are always talking about these people you know and I never knew if you were fibbing or not. I saw Crosby this morning and decided I'd find out if you really knew some of these people.

"I stepped up to Crosby when he came on the course and said...I'm looking for John Derr... and if he'd said he didn't know you, I'd know you had been blowing smoke."

What did he say, I asked her.

"He said he didn't know where you were but that you had eaten breakfast together today and you were wearing a brown jacket. Then he asked me if I would recognize you. I told him I thought I would – you were my brother."

I guess that told her. Fibbing? The very idea!!!

"What do you think about Rocky Marciano?" asked the NCO from the Armed Forces Radio Service. Sergeant Forino always called CBS Tuesday morning to learn what football game we were going to broadcast that he could send worldwide on AFRS.

"Who?" I asked.

"Marciano. Rocky Marciano. He's that good young boxer around Boston who is going to be great."

"He may be good around Boston, "I said, "but I've never heard of him. If he was any good I would know something about him."

"Well, the Boston papers write him up all the time." This sounded more like a plea than an observation. "Sergeant, he's probably just another local hotshot. I doubt if he could punch his way out of a paper bag. Our game this week is..."

Before I had finished my sentence there was the darnedest chatter coming in on the phone. The exchange of conversation told me that one or two extensions were in use.

"You see, Rocky, I told you nobody in New York believes you can fight. They laugh at me when I talk about you."

That was an aside at the point of origination. Now the voice came back to me. It sounded pained, seriously pained.

"John, someday you'll know who Rocky is. He's from my hometown. Rocky, meet John Derr and tell him who you've beaten in Brockton."

Now I remembered the name. I had heard of this young phenom. At CBS Sports we were always being told about great young boxers, great young golfers, great young pitchers, great young passers.

But I had called this boxer a nobody.

"Glad to meet you, Rocky," I carefully enunciated. "I was only kidding the sergeant about you being an unknown. Sure I know who you are and look forward to meeting you in person."

When I had finished groveling to the Brockton Bomber, he came on to assure me he knew I was kidding my Army friend.

Unless you are talking over the phone, from the safety of your own office a few miles away, it is not recommended that you tell a heavyweight boxer, who would soon become the champion of the world and who arguably was one of the five or six greatest in history – you don't say to him "he can't punch a lick."

A few months later I met Marciano at Toots Shor's and we had an enjoyable lunch. I had not intended to recall our phone meeting but Rocky brought it up.

"My buddy, Freddy Forino, thought it would be fun to have us meet over the phone the day he called you. Your answer rattled him." The best part of that luncheon was when Marciano reassured me that from the beginning he "knew I was kidding."

Even though I did the television commentary on perhaps a dozen world championship fights (no heavyweights) I got to know Marciano better than any other boxing champion. I was able to visit him several times in Brockton.

Coincidentally, on other business, I was in Brockton the day Rocky died in a plane crash. I never saw an entire town smother itself in mourning as Rocky's hometown did that day.

I, too, mourned the loss of a forgiving friend.

"As we advance the possible, the impossible shrinks. Three friends – Henry Ford, Harvey Firestone and Thomas A. Edison – were companions who hitched the gasoline engine to a buggy, cushioned the wheels to destructive road shocks, and lighted the road on the darkest night...All were great and daring believers. There is always 'great believing' on the line of great discovery."

--Ira Carney, Columbia, Iowa, philosopher.

SAIL ON, SAIL ON, O SHIP

The CBS color wheel was doing nicely. After months of controlled testing in the laboratory, the television industry had begun to take notice of the once-secret invention of Dr. Peter Goldmark. Television in color was here.

Using the rotating color disk, studio tests proved this contraption could produce true colors. Vibrant true colors. On a television receiving set, equipped with the proper converter the pictures were a sensational revelation.

Other industry scientists were also hard at work seeking a compatible product that could show color and/or black and white. It was a multi-million dollar race, the race to be first with a system that would have government approval and become the standard of the industry.

Dr. Goldmark had scored first and seemed about to win the battle for CBS. We were thrilled.

More testing was needed. The first outdoor test at Ebbets field vouched for the clarity of moving colors but that was a closed circuit experiment, no remote transmission.

Now it was time to take the equipment outside the studio, to actually telecast an event so its transmission qualities could be judged. The test event this time would be a horse race – the Molly Pitcher handicap from Monmouth Park race track on the coast of New Jersey.

This was to be a live broadcast. The signal would be beamed to New York and then down the line to Philadelphia and Washington.

There would not be a big audience – not big, but extremely important. Only some 10 sets were equipped with the requisite converters to show our color system.

Two of these would be in the CBS building at 485 Madison Avenue, one in master control and the other on the stage in the 20th (executive) floor viewing room.

Two other sets were placed in the storefront display windows at Macy's department store. There was always a crowd on the street there and they could stand on the sidewalk and see television in color – for the first time in public.

Two sets were likewise set up in Philadelphia, the ancestral home of CBS, where interest in this system ran high.

However, the four sets in Washington may have been the most important. They were located where they could be seen by selected Senators and Representative as well as members of the Federal Communications Commission, custodians of the airwaves. Their approval would be needed if the CBS system was to be the one chosen for the American public.

The sports department was called in to produce this event. To call the running of the race we brought in Joe H. Palmer, turf editor of the N.Y. Herald-Tribune and the most erudite race-caller in history. His native Kentucky drawl, polished by his career as a college professor, made him the ideal man to describe the race.

Judson Bailey, a former editor for the Associated Press and the top producer-director for CBS sports, was put in charge of production of the 30-minute program.

My assignment was to serve as host or emcee in conjunction with Palmer, whose forte was calling the right horses in the right order. This was no more difficult for his expertise than if he were doing it merely on the track public address system, but he was pleased to be on this first race colorcast.

As you know, race-callers identify the fast-moving thoroughbreds by the colors of the silks worn by the jockeys, as well as the numbers worn on the horses. For the first time in history television viewers would be able to distinguish the jockey colors themselves. Palmer always used only his binoculars to pick out the colors.

The program was to last 30 minutes, of which the actual race would be about two minutes. It was left to Bailey and me to use the other 28 minutes informatively and entertainingly. We had done this dozens of times but today, as they say at the race tracks, there was a change of equipment – no monitor in the announce booth.

We prepared a simulated script, a shot list as it were. As the events unfolded on our two lists, Bailey would punch up the picture and I would describe it. Describe it without seeing it.

The broadcast began at 4:00. The race was scheduled for 4:22 and the horses would be called from the paddock at 4:12 for their pre-race parade by the grandstand.

Promptly at 4:00 color burst forth in those few sets in Washington and elsewhere. It must have beautiful. Smiles beamed in the 20th floor viewing room, where television editors from the large daily newspapers, wire services and magazines had been invited to join the CBS high echelon to observe

At Monmouth the sun was shining. Early pictures showed the colorful crowd, milling about awaiting the next race. Some stood near the paddock for last minute study of the horses. Others, who knew their reasons for winning, lined up at the betting windows.

The infield was green with neatly trimmed grass and beds of colorful flowers dotted the landscape. Things never noticed took on new significance in color. The freshly-painted rails glistened. The running surface had been smoothed, like a sand bunker on a golf course. The sandy loam of the oval had a brilliance of its own in contrast to the more vibrant colors.

All seemed well at Monmouth. I talked about the track and its history, even explaining who was Molly Pitcher, the heroine from Revolutionary days for whom the stakes race was named. I was following our agreed upon loose script and very comfortable with the way things were going.

Then the reverberant sound of the bugle, calling the horses to the track, overrode the clamor of the crowd. Now for the first time we would specifically match picture and sound. This was my cue to describe the bugler, his uniform, his horn, his pageantry.

I referred to my notes to be sure I had the correct name of the lone musician. The notes helped me describe his colorful garments that might have been rejected by George Washington's tailor as being too dressy. This took more than a minute.

Unknown to me a drastic departure from script was going on from the control room. Just prior to this, while still showing generic pictures of the crowd and awaiting the bugler, Bailey's attention was distracted by a cameraman who had found an unplanned pretty bonus shot.

In scanning the horizon this camera had picked up a really pretty scene beyond the track. Only a few hundred yards off shore could be seen the billowing white sails of a pleasure craft easing its way down the New Jersey coast.

The wind was up and that meant the rolling white caps framed the ship as it raised up and lowered in the light blue waves under a sunny sky.

It was the kind of picture an alert cameraman loved. Colorful, moving and in its solitude a sharp contrast to the hubbub of the race crowds we had been showing.

Proud of his find the cameraman used his cue line to tell Bailey he had a really interesting picture to show him. A cue line is pretty noisy with voices from outside the control room and Bailey ignored the message. The cameraman called again, urging his camera be punched on the line. Okay.

However, in all the chatter, Bailey's ears were busy and he did not hear the bugle. He stayed on the quiet sailing ship. It was pretty and it added another element to our show.

Meanwhile the bugler was in full force. And so was I, telling about his tradition , his uniform and such. No mention was made of the ship which sailed blithely along its way.

The race was run without incident. Palmer handed the mike over to me and, buoyed by his fine call, a warmth of satisfaction was present in the booth as we said goodbye from Monmouth.

That was a feeling not shared elsewhere.

Harry Feeney of CBS Press Information, had arranged to have Peggy slip into the 20th floor room with the visiting press. She sat quietly in a rearward seat and watched her husband's historic telecast.

When I returned to my home in Upper Montclair that evening it was easy to see things had not gone as well as I thought.

"Did you see the broadcast?" Opened the conversation.

"Yes, and I thought you'd be fired before the race ended."

"Why, I thought it went well."

"Sit down and I'll tell you what happened."

This was her report:

"The first part went well. The color was good and the cameras showed the crowd and the track very favorably. Then when we heard the bugle you described the bugler and his red coat and brass bugle nicely...but the picture we were seeing was a ship, bobbing up and down in the bay."

"It was a beautiful picture, the ship, but you kept talking about the bugler and the horses coming on the track until you turned it over to Palmer. We all wondered what happened to the bugler and why you kept talking about him and not the ship."

Dr. Stanton (CBS President) was seated midway to the front. He called out in a brusque tone 'why doesn't Derr look at the monitor'?

Apparently no one answered him. At least we in the back didn't hear any response. This time Dr. Stanton gave an order, 'Get word to Derr to look at the monitor.' He sounded agitated.

Some one did answer now. He said you didn't have a monitor, that all the converters were in use on the demonstration sets.

"No monitor," Stanton said and repeated it.

" 'Don't ever do another broadcast when the announcer works without a monitor. Never. Never'." he emphasized. A weak 'yes sir' was heard.

"I know Dr. Stanton was furious but since it was not your fault you may not be fired, but he was pretty upset."

"At any rate, before they turned up the lights, I thanked Feeney and sneaked out the door and came home."

That was Peggy's tortuous report.

I wasn't fired, but the incompatibility of our color wheel with a black and white monitor—as seen by the FCC that day may have swung the government to withhold approval of a system that would essentially make obsolete thousands of current sets. They could have been modified at a small cost but it was a cost the FCC wanted to avoid.

The CBS color system was bypassed and millions of dollars went elsewhere, but color television had shown its value.

For want of a nail, the battle was lost.

For want of a monitor, millions were lost.

Nearly 50 years later (April, 1993) another color TV system was being tested and again I was lucky to be at the mike. This was HD-TV (High Definition TV) – a marvelously clear, ultra sharp system being tested.

Tokyo Broadcasting System, seeking USA approval of its equipment, brought HD-TV cameras and receivers to Augusta, where we covered Masters action of the 15th hole for two hours each day. One hole, one announcer.

Again it was for a limited but powerful audience. Receivers were placed in the clubhouse, press room and several cottages where FCC and Congressional types could observe the experimental Japanese system.

Since we had no tape of my television commentary, and because this was such an historic telecast, we asked if Tokyo could supply us with an hour's video.

When the TBS video arrived the sound track opened with happy Georgia birds singing away. Then nothing. Blank, like silent. In Japan where TBS sent the tapes, my carefully chosen words had been erased. Erased. Gone. Supply your own descriptive words.

"COMING TO THE DANCE"

When the SS America steamed past the Statue of Liberty and out of New York harbor in the afternoon of a July day in 1948, more than 500 of America's finest athletes were on board, heading for the London Olympics.

It was the last great voyage of our competitors going in the quest of gold. The four and a half days crossing the Atlantic gave the team members from the various sports a chance to get to know each other. Later Olympic teams flew to the sites and that social contact was denied them.

On that voyage the track stars got to know the basketball squad, the swimmers met the gymnasts and the water polo team got to know the rowing crews.

It also afforded the accompanying press and radio reporters an opportunity to do many background briefings, to become more familiar with the ladies and men we'd be talking or writing about during the next three weeks.

America's champion sculler, young Jack Kelly from Philadelphia, was considered a sure winner in this event. Sculling was one of many sports with which I was not too familiar and before we left New York a mutual friend wrote me a note of introduction to his father, John B. Kelly.

Mr. Kelly arranged for us to meet in one of the ship's lounges and when he showed up the entire family was with him, Jack, his mother and his teenage sister, Grace. I can't believe I ignored her but my focus was on her champion brother.

While Jack described for me the thrill and challenge of the lonely sport of sculling, I took notes on his training methods and tried to understand as much as I could to do a better job of explaining the challenge. Meanwhile the other Kellys drifted away from the lounge.

After broadcasting his victory at Henley, I met again with the celebrating family. The gold medal had been great revenge for the elder Kelly who had been snubbed when he sought a place on an earlier Olympic team. Everyone was in a joyous mood.

It would make a better story if I could say that this time I noticed the latent beauty in young Grace Kelly, but my only recollection of the moment was she had long legs and the cute childish happiness at brother Jack's achievement left her face wreathed in an attractive coyish smile. Nothing more.

My, how fast they grew up.

Six years later the little sister was the toast of the cinematic world, having won the "best actress" Oscar for her leading role in *The Country Girl.*

Back home in Philadelphia, friends planned an evening to honor their newest hometown heroine. Her "High Noon" had arrived.

George Jessel, America's celebrated

toastmaster general was to emcee the dinner. However, a week before the affair, George became ill when on tour in the Far East, leaving them in need of a substitute. Although numerous Hollywood celebs were coming, none volunteered to take Jessel's place.

Someone suggested my name but the date conflicted with a broadcast assignment and I declined the suggestion. A day or so later, Bob Levy called from Philadelphia and said he'd like to meet me for lunch the next day at Toots Shor's and he was bringing Grace along to convince me to change my plans.

The luncheon appointment was kept. Tourists and locals alike eyed the Oscar winner throughout the lunch. Toots had seated us at Table #2. He always reserved the first two tables inside the door, #1 on the right and #2 on the left, for his "biggest" name guests, patrons like Sinatra, DiMaggio or Musial. I had never sat at those tables.

Finally, convinced I could not attend, Levy left us to go to another appointment. Grace and I were having coffee.

Grace, preparing to leave, looked at her watch and gasped. It was later than she thought and she would be unable to catch the 3 o'clock train back to Philly. She'd have to wait until the next train, at 4 o'clock.

You can't leave a lady sitting alone in a restaurant, so we chatted another half hour. I put her in a cab and returned to my office...just another late lunch.

About noon the next day someone from the CBS Newsroom brought the early edition of *The N.Y. Journal American* to my office and said: "Well, I see you made Kilgallen's column."

He handed me the paper, folded to the column.

Halfway down, in her short notes style, it read: "Could it have been sports that Grace Kelly and John Derr were talking about while holding hands at Toots Shor's yesterday until mid-afternoon?"

Egad. We had not been holding hands. We had sat respectfully like other guests at a table. At once the thought flashed through my mind that Dorothy Kilgallen's syndicated column would appear the next day in the Miami newspaper and Peggy was in Miami, playing in the Helen Lee Doherty golf tournament.

Knowing a good offense beats a poor defense, a quick call was made to Florida for what I think they now call damage control.

"Be sure to read Kilgallen's column tomorrow," I told my bride, "but know there's not a word of truth in it." That only whetted her appetite so I read her the item.

And know this – the Kilgallen column, for the only time that winter, was not published next day in the Miami paper.

A decade or more later I was running the Jamaica Jamboree golf tournament in Montego Bay in the winter. We had pro-am teams from Europe, Canada and the United States. A team from France had a Spanish professional, Angel Gallardo, and the amateurs were three wealthy French counts.

Leader of the amateurs was Comte Guy de Bouisveray, whose family owned the tin mines of Bolivia. He had a winter home on the Tryall course. One day he told me he had house guests and would like to bring them to our gala ball at Round Hill.

Without asking who they were, I assured him we could add two places at his table and they would be most welcome.

"I believe you know them," he said. "They are Princess Grace and Prince Ranier. She tells me she's known you for some years."

The long-legged youngster of 1948, the Oscar winner of 1954 and the beautiful Royal Princess of 1963 was the hit of the ball. Some of our golf pros suffered eye strain that night.

The world lost a charming lady when she was the victim of an automobile crash a few years later. My times with her were minimal but my admiration for her was great.

Princesses are supposed to be beautiful and the beauty of Princess Grace was outstanding. I don't know how I could have ignored her at our mid-Atlantic first meeting.

From 1903 until 1951 every noted professional golfer in America included the North and South Open on his tournament schedule. It was truly a happening that no one dared miss.

For one thing it was played on a great course, No. 2; designed by Donald Ross who won that 1903 event. For another there was no hotel bill to pay. All contestants were guests of the Carolina Hotel.

And while the purse was meager, even by the standards of that day, the top eight finishers could count on winning gas money to get back to their club jobs up North.

In 1940 one of those hunting gas money was Ben Hogan.

He had almost tapped out in Florida and was about to accept an offer from Henry Picard for fluid for his Ford.

Hogan had never won an individual PGA event and here he was taking on Picard, Sarazen, Horton Smith, Hagen, Nelson, Demaret, Mangrum and the local favorite, Sam Snead.

For much of the way Snead led, but faltered near the end. When the last putt dropped it was the small, dark haired Texan who posted the lowest score. Victory at last. Pinehurst had become his favorite tournament, course and village.

After I watched the finish at 18, I left immediately for Greensboro, 75 miles away, to handle the office duties at the sports desk of The Greensboro Daily News.

Laurence Leonard, our golf expert, would write the story and send it up by Western Union. His report arrived and was sent to the composing room while I prepared the headline to go over the story.

The headline:

HOGAN CAPTURES NORTH-SOUTH OPEN.

We waited for the presses to roll out the first edition.

When we heard the hum of the big press it was the signal to go grab an early copy and check to see if there were errors.

I took one glance and screamed: "Stop the press!"

The headline:

HAGEN CAPTURES NORTH-SOUTH OPEN.

You should know the body of the story had been set in type by an operator on a linotype machine. At another machine another workman assembled the 48-point eight column headline. He had no knowledge of the contents of the story that would appear under the headline. He didn't need to. All he needed to know was to follow the copy he'd been given.

"Hey," I screamed, "can't you read English?" Having retrieved the original copy, I waved it in his face and told him it should read HOGAN not HAGEN.

His only comment..."Who's Hogan?"

He soon became familiar with Hogan in headlines.

Hogan followed that first-ever solo win at Pinehurst with a victory at Greensboro, went to Asheville the next week and won there...three in a row. Hogan had scored the Carolina Slam, the PGA Slam – Pinehurst, Greensboro, Asheville.

I made sure Hogan never saw the Hagen headline.

Nor heard about that question...Who's Hogan?

In the locker room of Atlanta's East Lake golf club, on a late October afternoon in 1944, tall, dark-haired, good looking Johnny Bulla, a world-class golf professional, rescued me from a possible manslaughter charge. I would have been guilty but it would have been Bulla's fault.

This had been a memorable day. Crisp autumn weather, not yet cold enough for a sweater. Only a few leaves remained on the fairways and no wind. With a few pars and pleasant companions, this would be "one of those days."

Bulla, a long-time friend of mine in Greensboro and a lifelong friend of golfing great Bob Jones was my partner. We were opposing Mr. Jones and a talented local amateur friend of his, Charles White..

The minor wagers were made and in total privacy we moved to the tee. Almost immediately fate handed me my most embarrassing moment in golf. I sliced wildly into the trees and here the leaves were plentiful. My caddie and I started looking. So did Bulla. So did White, and then I looked up and saw Emperor Jones, practically on his knees splashing the leaves aside, looking for my ball. Humiliation set in.

Now hurriedly let's get on with the play,

I urged. Forget my ball. I was happy to hear conversation begin between Bulla and Jones. Bob was asking about Bulla's known hobby of hypnotism. He asked what experiences Johnny had enjoyed with it.

"Once in Milwaukee," Bulla remarked, as we walked along, "I put Sam Snead under hypnosis. I had missed the cut and since Sam and I were driving together I would be hanging around a couple more days. I suggested Sam and I could try our talked about experiment in the third round. As Sam's caddie/coach I would hypnotize him and call the shots. Sam would execute. From the first tee. I directed his every swinging movement, even including the putts. Sam produced the easiest 65 you'll ever see."

Impressed but not convinced, Jones opined that hypnotism was interesting but he wasn't quite ready to try it. He asked Bulla if he could demonstrate it after we finished play. Bulla agreed. I knew what he had in mind. Several times before he had talked me under his spell. And here we go again, but nothing illegal, he promised.

After showering, Bulla began his explanation of how hypnosis works. Customary words were spoken, with customary compliance. Out of sight of the others, Bulla asked me to be sure Jones did not leave wearing Bulla's necktie. I understood. After dressing, Jones reached across to Bulla's locker, removed the necktie and slipped it around his neck. Wrong move.

"Not being disrespectful," I said, "Bob, I believe you're putting on the wrong tie. That's Johnny's tie." I laughed lightly. "May I have it, please?"

Jones kept tying, brushed me off and said "This is mine. Johnny's tie is still in the other locker."

I knew better. Bulla observed my attempt to retrieve the tie and appeared to urge me on. With one hand I grabbed the tie and with the other hand, I closed in on Bob's throat. He twisted and ducked. I squeezed it a bit more. I was determined. He would not leave with Bulla's tie.

At that moment, like every good hypnotist, Bulla snapped his fingers, the noise breaking my hypnotic trance. Relief and shock came to me, and maybe every one, at the same time. Here I had been choking the great Robert T. Jones in the locker room of his own East Lake golf course. What a mistake! OMG.

Bulla recovered his tie. Jones' neck only faintly sore. White was still laughing. For me, life's 2nd great embarrassment.

Did I mention the wagers had been paid much earlier? Mr. White had been relieved of four $1 bills, over to Mr. Bulla. With no fanfare, no spectators and cruelly (for me) no press photographers, Mr. Jones withdrew from his wallet four $1 bills. Timorously I accepted them, one by one. In my wildest fantasy, never would I win a wager from THE Bob Jones. I thanked him.

I wish now I had not spent them for beer.

Jones broke par that day at 71 and Mr. White was even with the card. Bulla's 66 was a thing of beauty and my 82 was good enough.

The best motto in golf is PPC.......Pick Partners Carefully.

Ione Davis patiently stood in the slow-moving line. She was about to apply for her marriage license. As happens, even with strangers, when time and lines move slowly, it helps to strike up a conversation with other reluctant standees.

The talkative, beaming young woman in front of Miss Davis grew vocally impatient as the creep-along line of future brides and grooms wended its way toward the clerk's desk.

After lamenting her discomfort, the woman asked, "What is your name?"
"Ione Davis."
"And what will your new name be?"
"Jones" was the one-word reply.
The woman repeated the name... "Jones, Jones. And your name now is Davis. You aren't really improving your name too much. You're not moving up ... Jones don't sound all that much more important tan Davis, but I guess you like it."

Undaunted by the doleful demeanor of the socially critical standee, Ione smiled and answered she was happy with the name.
"I'm not marrying him for his name but because I love him. And I happen to think he has a very attractive name -- Robert Trent Jones."

That name became one of the most recognized in golf and the former Ione Davis saw her new husband become the most widely celebrated golf course architect of his era.

Also, she became the mother of two sons who have enviable ranking among the world's best designers -- Robert T. (Bobby) and Rees Jones. She changed her name and helped make the new Jones family synonymous with golf design greatness.

I don't recall when first I met Trent, perhaps at a early Masters at Augusta, maybe the early fifties. Jones "held court" on the lawn under the trees or in the dining room of the old Partridge Inn near the Bon Air. He was much in demand.

There is no telling how many golf courses around the world had their designs imprinted on those all-day April outings in Augusta.

For many years Trent and I lived on the same street, several blocks apart. I made a pest of myself, visiting him often and asking him to help educate me on the intricacies of golf course design. When I would be televising a tournament on a course Jones had designed he would explain the whys and wherefores of certain holes. Then I could give an expert disclosure.

I think it was a result of these insights that Trent and I created a remarkably unsuccessful television program that was ten years ahead of its time. Called "Golf Challenge", it featured two professional golfers playing three holes (a 3,4,5) with a bonus award on every stroke. Commentary would be by Jones, the great Tommy Armour, and me.

Before each hole was played, Jones would describe the hole from an architectural point of view, select and point out on a map the exact location where the ball should go, according to the hole design. The player landing nearest that spot earned a cash bonus.

Armour, the Silver Scot, in his inimitable brogue, would elaborate on possible ways to play the next shot. After citing the various ways, Armour would tell his choice.

Describing how the players actually played the hole was my assignment. Thus we examined the game from the perspective of the architect, the profeessional player and the reporter.

Other bonus dollars were won by scoring eagles or birdies, sandies, chip-ins, winning the hole, etc. However, bonus money was subtracted if a player landed in the water or a sand bunker, three-putted or bogeyed the hole. The dollar winnings changed on very shot.

Winners stayed around to face a new challenger next week.

Jones was great in explaining nuances of the hole and Armour described more ways to play a shot than you ever imagined. Always after each hole Armour would immodestly tell how he would have conquered the hole. Jones persuaded him to join us and he was great. We never got on the air but during our rehearsals and filming I learned much about courses and shots.

"Golf Challenge" was another example of the ingenuity of Robert Trent Jones. We filmed one pilot at Pine Valley and another at Upper Montclair.

The pilot films were well received but this was in the 50's and golf had not reached the heights of popularity to which Eisenhower and Palmer would take it in the next decade. The fees were different too.

At one time Arnie was in our stable of pros, signed at a retainer of one dollar a year (but never executed... we couldn't sell the program).

No takers. We showed our film to companies and networks. Everybody liked it. No one would take the gamble on golf to sponsor it. Trent said it was good, somebody should buy it.

One day we heard from United Artists in Hollywood. They had read of our efforts in the trade papers and were willing to discuss distributing it. We met with their representative in New York and offered them 30% ownership for $300,000 and healthy contracts for Jones, Armour and me.

They took the offer west but weeks passed and no word. A call came from California. United Artists had decided to join our efforts and they would do the filming, selling, and distributing. We were to meet them Tuesday at the Waldorf, but Trent was in Spain, so I went with our lawyer.

"We have run through all the figures (today he would say he'd crunched them) and we believe we can make it fly. However, we can not invest the dollars this project will take -- money for filming, editing, promotion, salaries, etc.-- without United Artists having control of the project. That means we need 51%. You offered 30% for $300,000. We are prepared to pay you $500,000 for 51%."

Where was Trent when I needed him?
Unwise in big business, to me this half-million windfall sounded great, but when I located Jones in Spain he said... "No way. Tell 'em no."

"If we were to sell 51% we would lose control, not only the program idea but your name and reputation as well as mine. Not for half a million. Not for five million will I turn over my name to a motion picture company. "

I was "at liberty" as they say in show business and practically broke, but at Trent's direction I said "No" to Hollywood's offer.... Keep you $500,000... I can starve.

Cricket, you had a proverbial suntan as a new born baby, all because of the Joneses. There was a new instant camera on the market at that time, still quite new and costly. It was known as a Land Polaroid, named for Dr. Land, its inventor.

Among the gifts the Joneses brought for you was this newfangled instant camera. It was simple but not foolproof. An before Ione taught me how to use it I had wasted $50 worth of film. Eventually it worked, indoors and out. Flash bulbs exploded like New Year's Eve. Every visitor to our house wanted to try out this new camera and you were always the subject.

With two boys at her home, Ione looked upon you as their surrogate sister. She showered you with gifts and attention. She was as proud of you as though she'd hatched you herself.

And that lady from the long ago courthouse line, who told Ione she wasn't moving up in the world by changing her name from Davis to Jones can see the name-- Robert Trent Jones--- on hundreds of golf courses scattered across six continents.

That's moving up... all the way to the top.

Cricket, you won't remember this episode but you were an important part of it. Several years after your mother and I were married we decided it was time to start a family. No success. Friends used to say we'd been married 10 years and had nothing to show for it except two black cats, Timmie and his sister, Girl Kitty.

Late spring of 1956 Peggy went to Pinehurst to compete in the North-South Ladies golf tournament. She played well. The next week when packing to go to the Masters she decided not to accompany me. Without telling me why—we had experienced numerous disappointments – she suspected she might be pregnant, so opted to stay home and watch the first telecast of the Masters.

It was an exciting tournament, as most Masters are. Ken Venturi, an amateur, nearly won it after opening with a 66, but a last round 80 dropped him a stroke behind Jackie Burke, Jr.

The telecast had been well received. I did the 15th and 16th holes commentary and presided over the interviews by Cliff Roberts and Bob Jones with Burke and Venturi in the Butler cabin.

Monday was TV breakdown day and after a morning with the CBS engineering crew, I played Augusta Country Club with Eileen Stulb, an oft-time winner of the Georgia amateur crown.

Tuesday morning I packed my car and

drove to Augusta National Club for a courtesy meeting with Roberts, who by this time had heard reactions that would guide us in future years.

I sat with Mr. Roberts about half an hour and heard his generally favorable comments. Then Cliff looked at me and asked "where are your clubs?"

"In my car," I answered. "I'm about to drive to New Jersey and it takes about a day and a half."

Roberts said "Not so fast. You'd better go get your clubs and hit a few balls. President Eisenhower (who had arrived at Augusta Monday evening) has been on the practice range half an hour. He wants you to play with him this morning. He watched the telecast in Washington and wants to talk about it with you."

Panic set in. "I can't play, Cliff. I just learned last night that after all these years we are going to have a baby. It's important for me to get home. I can't stay here and play."

Roberts countered with, "I don't make the Chief's games. He asked me to have you play and if you won't you'll have to tell him."

What to do now?

Roberts continued, "He's fond of children and I'm sure he'll understand your excitement. But go get your clubs and you can beg off at the first tee."

What to do now?

With caddie and clubs I came to the course. Ed Dudley, the Augusta National professional, was talking with President Eisenhower and the fourth player, a Coca-Cola executive from Atlanta.

After greetings, I quietly sidled up to the President and explained my quandary.

"If I am to get home tomorrow (there were no interstates in those days) I'll need to leave by one o'clock. I could play nine, but then I'd have to hit the road."

"That's understandable," smiled the President. "Come on and play the front nine and we'll pick up someone at the turn."

What a relief.

That was about as much talking as we did. He rode in a cart with Dudley. We had four walking caddies and six Secret Service men in carts with live ammunition. A caravan.

Occasionally at the green he asked about the logistics of that first telecast but most of his conversation was with Dudley. He really was more interested in his game.

After nine I bade them good-bye and departed, humming an unfamiliar lullaby. There had been one disappointment. Since this was his first game in weeks, Eisenhower had requested that no press or photographers be permitted on the course. No pictures for posterity.

Within a few months, Eisenhower would be stricken with ileitis, requiring surgery and a long recovery. The country and the press wondered if the illness would negate his running for a second term. When his doctor, Lt.-General Leonard Heaton, told the press Ike's illness would not disqualify him, his hat was in the ring and he was re-elected in November.

Also in November there was a baby girl for the Derrs.

After the election, Eisenhower returned to Augusta for a much needed vacation. He wasted little time getting to the first tee and the next day he sent me a letter on stationery engraved Southern White House, Augusta, GA.

It said in part..."Congratulations on your new daughter. An unusual coincidence is that I heard the news on the first tee and it was at the first tee last April I learned of her anticipated arrival.

"Cliff did not know her name but I am sending her a memento medallion and you can have her name inscribed on it.

"Congratulations to you and your wife."

Dwight D. Eisenhower.

I thought about putting your name on the bronze bas-relief of the President – but I left it blank. You can do it now, Cricket, it's yours.

You will find it in the right rear corner of the

top drawer of my dresser. You can remember it's a reminder of the day you caused me to walk off Augusta National after playing nine holes with the President of the United States who had requested me to play with him.

In case you are wondering, I think I shot 41 and the President had no legit score, but I'd guess about 48.

Robert L. May, an employee of Montgomery Ward, was not the first advertising copywriter to ask for and be permitted to do his work at home. This, however, was probably the most popular and successful "home assignment" in history. It made history.

It was while babysitting his four-year old daughter, Barbara, that May first satisfied her plea to "tell me a story, Daddy." May learned that "working at home" was a multi-faceted chore. He continued to write advertising copy for the mail-order firm, continued to overlook the ramblings of Barbara and was seriously concerned about the illness of his wife, Evelyn, whose cancer had been classed as terminal. Times were tough.

May was successful as a writer but the pay was not too good. Living in a cramped apartment, with a seriously ill wife and a growing youngster, he asked permission to work at home and send his copy in by messenger. Permission granted, although in 1939, such arrangements were rare. Bob would attend to his duties until late in the afternoon when a "played out" Barbara would make her request known. "Tell me a story, Daddy."

Animals were the native New Englander's childhood heroes so it was only natural that Bob's stories for Barbara would be about animals, more particularly about one breed, reindeer. Instead of a narrative, he wrote her stories in poetic couplets. Writing was his business and these diversions for Barbara offered him much pleasure and distance from his advertising copy. When Bob found time he would pen three or four escapades.

Several names were tested to identify the reindeer before he settled on Rudolph. And when one of the episodes had Santa Claus fearful the fog would stop his trip until he decided to use the red nose to light the way, that was how the critter became Rudolph, the Red Nosed Reindeer.

In Montgomery Ward stores each Christmas a free pamphlet-like story was distributed as a promotion item for the children who came to see Santa Claus. Usually Ward bought a generic story, but when fellow writers heard May's stories for little Barbara, they suggested those stories would be a better give-away for the youngsters. Not only were they new and original but they could be expanded and become an annual tradition. Since May had written the stories while on company time, they were already owned by Wards, another selling point.

A copywriter colleague in the advertising department, Miss Dorothy Adams, led the office campaign for Rudolph. She had read many of the stories and been impressed with Bob's creations for Barbara. Why wouldn't they appeal to the hundreds of children who would visit the Ward stores during the holidays to see Santa Claus?

Was Rudolph a hit? Those 1939 youngsters

claimed all of the 2.5 million copies and his popularity grew. The story became a Ward's holiday feature for years and eventually the circulation of popular Rudolph exceeded six million. This became the biggest promotion of its type ever distributed for children.

Appreciating the success and magnitude of the advertising venture, May was assigned the authorship rights by the company. This permitted him to gain some financial benefit for his creative little couplets, even to having them published for commercial consumption. Rudolph developed a following during the early years of WWII and among the fans was Bob May's brother-in-law, Johnny Marks.

A successful songwriter and recording artist, Mr. Marks revised the story and came up with the musical version of Rudolph. It is alleged that Crosby and other singers turned it down. Just another of the thousands of rejected songs, it appeared. Then it was offered to the singing cowboy, Gene Autry. For him it was a tremendous hit and sold millions of records, second behind "White Christmas" of all Christmas songs.

Meanwhile there was more to come. By 1964 Dorothy Adams, from her desk next to Bob May in Chicago, had advanced to New York and was now an Account Executive at the Maxon Advertising Agency. She was in charge of the General Electric Housewares Division account, responsible for offering GE wares to the public in a multi-million dollar budget. During conferences with GE executives as to what type television program might get the best audience response, Miss Adams remembered the excitement caused 15 years earlier by Ward's promotion featuring that misfit reindeer, Rudolph, with the flaming red nose.

During a client-agency conference Adams described her recollection of Rudolph, explaining the creation of the lovable little misfit and how the innovative story had produced maximum promotion and sales. This was what GE was hunting and the story board was approved by the client, an exciting first step. Rudolph was about to enjoy a rebirth and he was only 15 years old.

Arrangements began for the filming of character-set drawings for the television network debut of Rudolph. As an assistant to Miss Adams, I was involved in the promotion of the TV Rudolph. My job was to learn and tell about his beginning and secure an audience for his debut. This afforded me many informative sessions with Mays and Marks.

Bob May turned out to be a conservatively shy but very cooperative gentleman. Through lunches, conferences and chatter in the production room I got to know a lot about Rudolph and how Bob came to bring him to life. Bob was as modest as any successful author could be and I liked him better when I learned he was an avid golfer, but not too good. Around the studio, we told golf tales and I made a promise. I would be announcing the PGA tournament from the Tam

O'Shanter club in Chicago in six months and I'd have Bob as a guest on my television tower. The anticipation in Bob's eyes sparkled brighter than a certain red nose.

In August, Bob met me at the course and away we went. I wanted him to meet and shake hands with Sam Snead, Ben Hogan and Byron Nelson. No kid in a candy store was ever happier. Through the day, Bob drank it all in from the tower as he sat by my place at the table. And then he asked how about tomorrow.

He was on hand early the next day and greeted me with this:
"I wanted to check again to see if I had one left. I do. This means you will soon get a leather-bound, gold-leaf copy of the publisher's first edition miniature of Rudolph, the Red Nosed Reindeer. It is a numbered limited edition and I am pleased to sign it for you."

His flattering inscription closes with this :
"from Rudolph's old man."

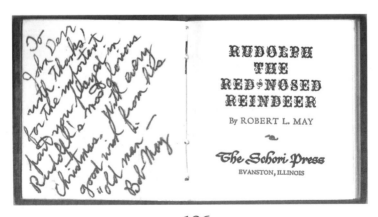

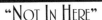

During a Sunday lull in the 1948 Olympics, Peggy and I accepted an invitation from Eric Brown, a British friend I had known in New Delhi, to visit him at his home in Tunbridge Wells and play golf at his home club.

The early morning train from London fairly flew along the tracks, easing its way through the morning fog that festooned the English countryside. Riding an English train in the early morning can be a pleasurable experience – but at night, as we learned this day, it can be quite different.

Eric met our train, loaded the clubs in the rumble-seat of his little pre-war roadster and we headed for the course.

En route Eric had some words of caution.

Not only had this part of England been a target of German bombers and the cross-channel buzz bombs, but Allied bombers returning from a raid with unfired bombs found the golf course a fitting place to jettison their live ammunition.

"You will find a lot of craters around the course. If you happen to put a ball in a crater and can see it, retrieve it very carefully. Don't try to play it. There are unexploded munitions in the ground and if your club happened to make contact we might have a deadly explosion."

Not your typical explosion from a hazard.

The short course was quite playable but all the reminders of what had taken place there just a couple of years earlier created a somber ambience throughout the round.

This was more underscored when we noticed a row of three white wooden crosses in the rough, 20 yards from the 15ᵗʰ green.

Eric explained. "The crosses mark the graves of three Nazi flyers who were shot down here during the war. Local people buried them right where they fell. That might seem inhumane but remember there was a war going on."

After golf, Eric took us to the home of a friend, the biggest sheepherder in the Falkland Islands, and we were served a delicacy in post-war England, real chicken salad.

We visited too long. Eric was startled when he looked at his watch and warned we had 10 minutes before the last train of the night left for London. We raced but didn't make it, the last car was disappearing down the track.

Eric tried to calm our panic by saying he knew a short cut and we could catch it in a neighboring town. I never knew a short cut that was shorter than the straight lines of a railroad and this one wasn't either.

We did get there while the train was stopped. Out came the clubs and we ran, yelling our good-byes en route. There was movement of the train but no passenger coach with an open door.

"Here's one," Peggy called to me as I trailed with the clubs. Up she jumped into what looked like a box car. I tossed in the clubs and ran along until I got up enough speed to swing up into the moving hole. With a final lurch I made it.

As I tried to pick myself up from the floor I looked straight into the barrel of the biggest pistol I had ever seen.

This persuaded me to stay laying down.

"You can't come in here," shouted the man with the weapon, and all the time I thought British didn't carry weapons. This is not a passenger coach. This is the Royal Mail car."

Whoa...we jumped into trouble.

Again our unwilling host said we could not ride in the mail car. But he didn't seem like the kind of fellow who would push us out the door of a moving train. His concern now was what we had in those golf bags.

With his lighted torch he examined each of our light "Sunday bags" and I don't think he was checking the grooves of the irons.

After he was convinced we were not armed he allowed us to sit on our bags until we got to the next station. There he opened the door and assisted us and our clubs to the platform.

We dashed back to a coach and headed for London – our ride in the Royal Mail car happily at an end.

As though to emphasize our good fortune at having met a friendly postal clerk, he still had the last word, shouted to us as we departed... "I told you you can't ride in here."

For a time we thought our little white crosses might be nailed to the floor of the Royal Mail car.

A PAINLESS DENTIST

When your golf TV coverage ends, most listeners have no concern for where the announcing crew goes. Today's boys in the booth usually scatter in all directions to their own pursuits. I'm grateful that in the early days of golf television, even though our crew had been orally connected and physically separated all afternoon, we often shared tea time and dinner afterwards. What happened at one of these dinners in Detroit causes me to vote professional golf champion, Dr. Cary Middlecoff, my all time MVP announcer/ dentist.

In order for me to have any voice left for Saturday and Sunday broadcasts it was necessary to take medications Friday night for what was thought to be a strep throat. On this night Ray Scott asked if my throat was getting any better. The answer was negative. Seated across the table from me was the former Army dentist, twice winner of the US Open, owner of a 1955 Masters Green Jacket and a drawer full of rusting dental tools. He now shared his golfing knowledge over the air with us and millions of TV viewers. A real pro, thrice over.

"How long has this croaky throat been bothering you ?" Cary asked.

About three weeks, I answered, drawing a frown from the good doctor.

"I heard you say your doctor prescribed medication you take before the telecasts, medicine which soothes your throat so you can speak, but only for a day or so. Right? When does he expect this infection to be cured?"

There was no answer, no forecast. At this point, Dr. Middlecoff said "obviously you have an infection somewhere in your body. I don't know where it is. I don't know that it's in your throat, although it may be. Has your doctor checked you for a kidney infection or an infection anywhere else in your system?"

I wondered why would a dentist ask such a question. Then he said "your doctor should check your kidneys. Just because a throat is irritated doesn't mean that that's where the infection is. Your body has an infection somewhere and your doctor should be able to find it. Because you use your throat so much it just may mean the infection has settled there but it may be elsewhere in your system."

Three days later, after I had seen my doctor in Montclair, the cultures revealed that indeed, the infection was in my kidneys. Medication was begun and within eight days my throat had cleared up. There had never been a strep throat. I changed doctors, hunting one who pulled teeth and could putt.

My golfing dentist, who spent many months in the Army pulling teeth had pulled from his magical experiences a suggestion that perhaps my problem was not in my throat. He was correct. That kidney infection for three weeks had been getting worse and worse. If undetected, there was no telling how long it, or I, may have lasted. So perhaps his suggestion saved my life and he didn't even send me a bill. That's what I call a good doctor... a painless doctor.

But Middlecoff, the golfer, was special. too.

In 1945, while still wearing his military uniform, Lt. Middlecoff entered the North and South Open at Pinehurst. It was an open event but he played as an amateur. He fought his way to total victory and in case you may have thought he beat a bunch of nobodies, when he walked up the 18th fairway of the Pinehurst No. 2 Course, alongside of him were two notable beaten competitors, champions in their own right--- a couple of fellows named Gene Sarazen and Ben Hogan.

Middlecoff won the Open at Medinah in 1949 and again in 1956. He also tied in 1957, a hot streak. At Medinah, one hole stood out in Cary's planned pursuit. This was the par 5 No.14 hole, some 510 yards in length. The long hitting Middlecoff thought he should be able to reach it in two and grab perhaps an eagle, or certainly a few birdies. In round one he drove well, set up for the shot to the green but the ball wavered to the right and landed in the right-side bunker. Missed putt. No birdie.

In round two. He drove well again, set up for

the shot to the green but this time the ball landed in the other bunker. No birdie, just another par. Now in round three, the first of two rounds on Saturday, Cary elected once more to try to reach the tantalizing green and get his eagle. No luck again. Frustration about now.

In the afternoon, his fourth round, Doc was still very much in contention for the title, but it was time to change tactics. Cary elected to play short, forget about going for the green in two. He left himself an easy pitch, some 75 yards, to the green. The pitch he executed perfectly, sank the birdie putt and had his winning score. A lesson learned. Yards are only part of the equation.

Being in the field of champions...fellows like Hogan, Snead, Nelson, Demaret, and many other good players... did not keep Dr. Middlecoff from winning many times during the 50's decade. His next major was in 1955 Masters and once more there was a single hole he could point to as the turning point of his win. In the second round, Cary pulled ahead largely because of the 13th hole, a par five over Rae's Creek. His long iron second cleared the water but barely stayed on the green, it rolled far back to the right hand corner. The pin had been cut on the very front, a long distance away. After much study, and Cary was not a fast player, he eventually settled down to putt. It seemed like several minutes, and once the ball started rolling someone timed it at 7 seconds to the cup. It seemed minutes. A long way. Yes, it was measured at 86 feet. Bob Jones, who from his motorized cart was watching, said it was the longest meaningful putt thus far seen at Augusta.....86 feet. Have you an idea of how long is 86 feet? Try it sometime.

This was one very important stroke but it was not necessarily the winning one, because Dr. Cary Middlecoff, late of Tennessee, late of the Army Dental Corp, won that Masters by seven strokes over Ben Hogan. When he reached a green, he must have remembered an oft-heard plea by dentists. He asked the cups: "Open Wide."

One other unforgettable episode with the golfing dentist took place during a PGA telecast in Tampa. The network arranged to cover our announce tower with a heavy tarpaulin to protect us, mainly from the sun. As it turned out, it rained about an hour into the show. A semi-tropical rainstorm hit us and our fabric overhead roof began to sag. Rain caused the middle to drop lower, lower, lower and lower.

Cary, standing well over 6 feet moved his chair to the center of our platform in the sky pushed up on the heavy tarp. It was heavy and hardly moved. With new vigor, my professional partner pushed up. Strong. And swosh! Water, water. A non-scheduled flood.

We were on the air at the time and did not realize that when the water flowed over the edge of the tarp, it would belly under and come back inside on us. We were soaked. Our papers were soggy. Our fancy TV clothes were drooping. Doc missed the diagnosis on that move, but I loved him, wet clothes and all.

Middlecoff's golfing career was at its highest when some of golf's greatest players were teeing it up every Thursday. He seldom got credit for being as great a golfer as he was. Look at his record. Better still, read his books, if you can find them.

Like him, they are great. Days with Doc were fun.

He wanted to see – not be seen.

He wanted to hear – not be heard.

He was a perfect companion on a television tower.

Joe DiMaggio was seated alongside me on many Saturdays and Sundays when I was televising PGA tournament action from the tower behind the 17th green.

Sports television pioneer Dick Bailey, president of the Hughes Sports Network, was a friend and business associate of DiMaggio and would bring the Yankee star to tournaments.

Sometimes he would play in the pro-am with the sponsors on Wednesday and always acquire a large crowd of fans. Then on Thursday and Friday Joe would slip off to another club and play with friends. Occasionally I would fill in.

On Saturdays and Sundays Joe would climb the ladder to my tower, pull up a folding chair and quietly observe the play from our vantage point of 20 feet or more up above the green. He could see a great deal more from there than he could from any ground location – plus at 20 feet up he knew there would be no crushing crowd seeking autographs.

I don't think at the time I appreciated what an unusual and outstanding hero he was. I now deem him to have been America's greatest sports hero – with class. And did he have class?

DiMaggio was a baseball hero, a Yankee hero, an American hero when loyalty meant something and was more than a little-used word in the dictionary. You didn't have to define it. You knew.

Fans were loyal to the players;

players were loyal to the owners;

and owners were loyal to the fans and home towns.

In those golden days of sport we thought there was enough honor and loyalty to last forever. It disappeared and loyalty was replaced by a word meaning greed. Grab it and run. Most of the latter-day athletes, blinded by dollar signs, showed no loyalty to teams or towns, family or friends.

DiMaggio was different. He had a disabling bone spur in his heel but under his feet sat the pedestal he deserved.

Maybe the reason I was not in awe of this great athlete was because he was so at ease being "an ordinary Joe." He gave away a million autographs...to kids, their dads and their granddads. Joe was a natural hero to all ages.

Cricket, you asked me to recall some of the people who had helped me get along through life. DiMaggio was one of those who impressed me with the casual manner he accepted greatness. I had known others who were great and many who thought they deserved that ranking but none with Joe's elegance.

He was kind.

Often when we were walking in public, fans would descend on him and try to get into a conversation. Sometimes an autograph would suffice but many wanted to talk. This was true of men whose wives were with them. It made them feel close to greatness.

Never once did I see him "brush off" a sober fan but he had no time for the inebriated ones. He would recall his swift technique for running down a ball in center field and he'd disappear into the crowd. I'd be there a few seconds later.

Three baseball seasons (1943-44-45) he lost while in military service in World War II. Twice before, in 1939 and 1941, he had been the Most Valuable Player in the American League and he gained that honor again after service, in 1947.

Joe never complained about losing three seasons which could have been his most productive. One hates to think how players of the last decade of the century would have reacted to such interference with their multi-million dollar livelihood. They, or their bevy of agents, would probably have sued the War Department.

When we were on the tower during play there wasn't much opportunity for conversation, but Joe was a good story-teller and a charismatic companion. I remember one tournament, I think it was at Doral, when my back had been especially painful and I had deadened it with codeine medicine. Joe said they should give me an Emmy award for sounding so happy on the air but being in such pain that I cried like a baby when we'd closed out our part of the telecast. He helped me in many ways.

I think I saw the driving force of DiMaggio's life one day when we were playing golf at Pinehurst. It was clear where his priorities were. I wish I could have helped him as he did me, but there was a satisfying loneliness in his demeanor that I did not feel privileged enough to penetrate.

We were on the No. 5 course. We drove from the 8th tee, and as we went to get into the golf cart, Joe said, "If I could live at Pinehurst, I would want a house right there," pointing to a wooded triangular lot, facing west, that separated the fifth tee from the eighth green.

It was not a location I would have picked. Not near an entrance road, lots of pine trees that would discourage a lawn and the view of the very ordinary eighth green was just so-so.

"Why there?" I asked Joe.

He already knew why and didn't have to think for an answer.

"It's quiet."

I learned much from this tall handsome great American hero. For him, quietness was next to Godliness. To me, so was DiMaggio.

Off in the distance the bands were playing and a wisp of a breeze blew the sound all the way to Bay Front Park where the crowd had gathered to see another spectacular Orange Bowl Parade.

The year was 1952, late December, a peaceful time. The nation had survived a long contentious political campaign and elected a popular war hero president. It had also elected a California senator as vice-president, and Richard M. Nixon had accepted an Orange Bowl bid to be the politician of honor and review the parade.

Temporary reviewing stands had been erected at the foot of Biscayne Boulevard and the reserved seats began to fill long before the parade was scheduled to arrive.

The long wooden third row was reserved for what they called the "official party." As the representative from CBS, I was told my seat was on the left side of that row, alongside the Oklahoma and Maryland school presidents and coaches.

Four seats in the center of the row were left vacant until the arrival of the vice president-elect, Mr. Nixon.

Before his party arrived a ranking official of the Orange Bowl came to my seat and with an air of importance told me that when Mr. Nixon arrived he would take me over to meet him. This would have meant a dozen dignitaries, whose seats were between his and mine, would have to stand or run the risk of being clumsily stepped on.

"Never mind," I told him. "It's too much bother to do it here. I will meet him again some time later."

This did not please my Orange Bowl friend, who I think saw this as a chance to enhance his already well developed ego, by showing that he knew the visitor well enough to introduce him to a friend. He was insistent.

Somewhat discourteously, I fear, I finally said, "Really I don't care to meet him. If he wants to meet me, bring him over here."

Our conversation was heard by those around us.

A few minutes later a gentleman tapped me on the shoulder, suggesting I stand, and asked if he could have a word with me.

He pulled open the lapel of his coat to show me he was a Secret Service agent.

"I understand you want to meet Mr. Nixon but don't want to inconvenience the other guests."

"No," I said. "I don't care to meet the vice president-elect. Someone misinformed you. I'm perfectly fine here."

Seeming perplexed by my comments the agent returned to street level as the Nixon limo was stopping at the far end of the stands.

The Nixon party arrived, along with the president of the Orange Bowl. Introductions were made to those seated nearest him and the first floats rolled into view.

As always, the floats were spectacular and the bands played with normal enthusiasm and loudness. The floats continued.

Thirty minutes into the parade the original Secret Service agent returned and introduced me to the senior agent in charge. He had the same intention, only more forceful.

"When the last float goes by," he told me, "I'll come here and lead you down the steps and over in front of the reviewing stand and when Mr. Nixon comes to his car I'll introduce you."

Without so much as a nod of understanding the senior agent said he'd be back to lead me down the steps.

The Queen's float arrived, paused and then rolled on up the boulevard.

We had been told to remain seated until the Nixon party moved out. Every one did until that agent came back and beckoned me to come with him. On the other end of the row the Nixon's had started out.

Down the steps to the street, across to the limo and we arrived at the same time as the Nixons.

The agent said my name and Nixon extended

his hand.

"I'm glad to meet you, John," showing a politician's skill at quick recall of names.

"When have you seen Basil Whitener?" he asked.

Not in months, I answered, since I was based in New York and Whitener was a Democrat congressman from North Carolina and spent his time in Washington.

Nixon got in his car and disappeared up Biscayne and I was faced with a first class mystery. How had he known I knew Basil Whitener? Was he really that knowledgeable about everyone?

Months went by, even a couple of years and the mystery faded away. Occasionally I would ask some politician about it but no one had an answer.

Then one night at the New York Athletic Club on the occasion of the naming of the Heisman football award winner, Nixon was the featured speaker. At the backstage reception he came by and shook hands.

"This time you didn't ask about Basil Whitener, why?"

He didn't recall the Miami meeting until I reminded him he had asked when I had seen Whitener.

"How did you know Whitener was a friend of

mine?" I asked

"The FBI told me," he chuckled. "You were so insistent that you did not want to meet me that night it aroused their suspicion that there may have been more to it than that.

"They ran your name through the FBI files, together with mine to seek a common connection. They found you were on a basketball team with Basil and he was a supporting sponsor of your appointment as a special agent during the war.

"Basil and I were in the same law class at Duke.

"When they found a common acquaintance they messaged Whitener's name to Miami and the agents there were watching your reaction and recognition factor when I mentioned his name."

I've forgotten who won that Heisman. I left the hall knowing that "big brother is really watching."

Now I'm pleased and willing to meet everyone.

In the late spring of 1947, professional golfer Sam Snead arrived at New York's Idlewild airport with a couple of visitors from South Africa. A cable from Sam two days earlier, asked me to meet him at the airport, in a large car. He didn't want to use a cab or public transportation. A king-size sedan was borrowed to bring his party to a Manhattan hotel.

One of his visitors was a 2- pound South African native animal, a little varmint, something like a baby squirrel, that Snead called a "*nocht apus.*" The other visitor was a full-sized South African golfer, who was enjoying civilian life after recently spending 2,000 hours in a World War II bomber over Europe. He was Arthur D. 'Bobby' Locke. His very first question to me as we arrived in Manhattan was ... "Which is the Great White Way? I have heard of it for years. "

Unknown to American golfers that night, his eyes aglow and speaking in his unique rolling burr, Locke brought a new name, a new game to golf. He would soon be an exciting new star on our PGA tour. Let me explain Snead's other guest. Sam was attracted to his little "night ape" because African friends told him it would make a great pet back in Virginia. Using the left sleeve of his light topcoat as a carrying case, Snead eased through customs and left the baggage collection for me. Sam got his pet home to Hot Springs the next day but" N A" was not meant to be a pet. After a few weeks, he was allowed to escape. Sam's neighbors remarked that occasionally they'd seen a funny looking squirrel among his trees. Sam never explained.

Nor could Sam explain how he had lost 12 of the 14 matches he played against Locke in South Africa, Snead's exhibition tour had been arranged by his manager, Fred Corcoran, golf's great promoter. The Virginian had been expected to win, maybe every match, but when Locke smashed Sam, Corcoran saw a new client fall into his lap. Corcoran made sure that Mr. Locke would get his chance to play here. Locke made his American debut at the 1947 Masters, only a few days later. He tied for 14th and won $188. Host Bob Jones was his first round companion.

Locke became very popular with the American golf fans, but not so much with the PGA Tour players against whom he teed it up every week. The dapper Locke was easy to recognize on the course. He dressed in solid gray or black flannel knickers, a white linen shirt, a solid color plain necktie- -always wearing a tie- -and the flat smallish cap, also white, much like Hogan's custom-made headgear. Locke's unique swing could be identified from anywhere on the course. He had a calculated slow bend to the left on almost every shot.

Being unfamiliar with the ways in America, Locke heard a different drummer in his band. For instance, after he won a handful of PGA tournaments he was highly expected to win the 1947 United States Open in St. Louis. He was the subject of many magazine and newspaper columns. *Time* magazine, elite of the elite nonsporting magazines, contracted with its famous cover artist, at a fee of $5,000, to do a cover featuring Bobby. No one ever turned down the cover of *Time*, but when the magazine representative finally had a conference with the new star, he was dumbfounded. Locke asked "What will be my fee?"

It was explained to him the cover of *Time* was not for sale. How many pros would have jumped through the hoop for that public recognition? Friends tried to tell him he was overlooking something that money couldn't buy, but Mr. Locke had his price. No cover.

There was much to admire about the game of our guest but most attention was paid to his putting. He was a great putter. After he addressed the ball, he moved the putter slowly and widely, arcing to his side. He eased open the blade a bit, ever so slightly. At the same speed he continued his backswing. On the return swing, Locke appeared to direct his club to the right of a normal putting line. In this way he played a rolling hook.... every putt. And he made almost every one.... Don't try it. You're no Locke.

Locke didn't win the 1947 Open. Neither did Snead, the other favorite to capture the only major he missed. This could have been Snead's day. He sank an 18- foot putt on the 72nd hole to tie Lew Worsham. Still even after 17 playoff holes, Worsham asked that their putts be measured to determine the order of play. Snead was barely away, missed his putt. Worsham then sank and won the $2,000 first prize. Each got an extra $500 for the playoff round.

Locke resumed his triumphant tour of America, being the subject of story after story in the press. "The Key to Locke" was the title one magazine put on a story I wrote. I opined his success was beginning to get under the skin of competitors like Jimmy Demaret, Lloyd Mangrum, Porky Oliver and a handful of really good players.

One at a time they would, usually in the locker room, offer a wager with Locke on that day's play. Not too big. But enough to get his attention. Then another player would snag Bobby. Another bet, maybe the same size. And some days Locke would have accepted as many as four or five bets. One at a time. The other bettors had only one check riding on a 12- foot putt. Locke had maybe six or seven, so the pressure mounted in proportion. And in time he would falter. These were private wagers, possibly made collectively, but it was the pressure that got to the foreigner.

Despite the gamesmanship pressure, Locke continued successfully for another couple of years. The visitor who came and stayed, played 59 PGA events and won 11 of them, was second in 10 others and 8 times was third. One might have thought he was the forerunner of a later day star named Tiger Woods, finishing in the top 3 places

29 times out of 59. Neat.

When he arrived here after his stomping of Snead back home, Locke did not possess a sand iron. He had never used a deep throated wedge. For a couple of weeks he was a guest of Dugan Aycock, the Lexington, North Carolina, professional, whose 18th hole at his club was flanked by two huge bunkers. Dugan gave Bobby three styles of wedges and told him to start tossing sand. He wore out two as he moved that sand, up and down, up and out, hour by hour. Locke became almost as good with the wedge as with his trademark shiny silver-toned South African magic putter.

Aycock invited his guest to compete in the Championship of the Carolinas PGA, a section Aycock served as president for many terms. Locke won it. And then the next year he came back off the big tour to show his appreciation, and he won it again. "Putted like a demon" said some of the Carolina players, who offered him a return ticket. A return ticket home, that is.

Gary Player claimed he played 100 rounds with Locke in South Africa and could recall only once that he took three putts on the green. It was hook 'em, sink 'em. Bobby.

After a contentious controversy in 1949, Locke lost his privileges to play on the American PGA Tour. It was said he had agreed to play a certain number of tournaments in this country but had gone to play in Europe. During this time there he won his first British Open and elected not to come back to play the American tour. He never again competed here as a regular. Locke won 4 British Opens in a span of eight years. He won the Open in 1952, the year before Hogan and again in 1954. Badly injured in an automobile accident a few years later Locke never resumed his golfing career. He died in 1987 at his home in Johannesburg, South Africa. He was 69, a friendly but reserved and untrusting personality.

With that great record in a short career, one would have thought the golfing world would better remember the big gruff South African, who hooked every putt he played. And holed most of them. Television might have made him more popular if his skills had been seen more but think of the host of players who would have given up the game --- after trying to hook their putts.

The summer you were 11 you had a lot of ups and downs. We vanned your horses to Maine that year. In the evenings your mother and I would sit on the porch and watch you and neighbor Nancy race around the big paddock, playing hide-and-seek on horseback.

You entered the 4-H horse show at the Fryeburg Fair Grounds and although younger than most other entrants you rode well. You snared a couple of placing ribbons but no victory. The last event was the one for which you had trained hard and well.

While we awaited the decision, the judge called four of you back into the ring for another look to reinforce his evaluation. Go right, go left, stand. He continued to look. Then he pinned the class. Alas, you were placed second.

The fact the winner and the judge lived in the same little community, as we learned during the event, was just one of those unfortunate coincidences that happens at local horse shows. We chose not to say what others told you...that you were robbed.

On the way home I talked about the valleys and mountains we face...in life...in sports...in work. One has to accept the valleys between the mountains, the bad between the good, maybe a lesser ribbon or no ribbon at all some days. Your disappointment resisted but you accepted the theory.

That you did understand came to light a few weeks later when you competed in the "greased pig" contest at the Fair. Some 35-40 youngsters stood at the end of an oblong pen. At the other end, restrained in crates, were a dozen piglets. They had been coated with lard and were as slippery as eels.

On the signal, the pigs were released. Then you kids were released. Anyone who could hang on and get the pig back to the crates, could keep his or her prize. We did not say "good luck."

This would be quite a prize for the farm boys and girls but we were less enthusiastic about becoming pig grandparents.

The great roundup began amidst much squealing, some by the piglets. Grab one and he'd slip away, good. Then it happened. You had one by the front leg and were pulling it toward the line, nearer and nearer you dragged him.

Beside you a young boy seemed to have his squealer in tow. All of a sudden his pig bolted, hit your pig and both went free. Relief for two observers.

Before you could lay hands on another greased pig all of them had been corralled. No more pigs. Disappointed, you came to us and we drove home...without a pig...but with a very dejected young lady.

"I had him right there until that boy let his

pig get loose and he ran into mine. I'm sure I'd have won him," you lamented. You bit your lip and tried to be brave but when we got to our home the tears rolled down your cheeks.

Again I tried to console you, reminding you of our earlier discussions about the ups and downs, mountains and valleys.

I had to turn my head and mask a wee smile when you dried your eyes, sniffled a bit and replied: "But, Daddy, I've had more valleys lately than one little girl can stand."

You were reminded that valleys don't follow valleys. Next to valleys are hills and mountains. Every mountain has a peak.

Keep up your spirits, so you can enjoy your next climb.

By looking ahead you can see the path and remember, as you put one foot in front of the other, going uphill is easier, for when you cross that peak each step down accesses the valley.

And uphill is definitely easier...without the pig.

The first year CBS televised the Masters in color I spent $18.00 to have our year-old set adjusted. I tried to do it but the greens were red and the reds came out as blues.

Knowing how beautiful was the Augusta National in person I sensed the azaleas on color TV would be spectacular.

When I returned from Augusta, I asked if you liked the colored flowers at the 13th hole.

"I didn't see 'em, Daddy," you confessed.

Here I'd spent $18 to have the color adjusted and no one watched. Your mother had told me she watched on black and white in the bedroom. Now you tell me you didn't see it on any set.

"Why?" I asked.

"Daddy, I heard your broadcast. I just didn't see it."

I might as well have been doing it on radio.

Again I asked you why, becoming somewhat irritated that in my own house, the first colorcast from Augusta was ignored.

You were probably about nine years old at the time.

"I'll tell you, Daddy. I was playing in the sun room with Rachel Watson, my friend from school. So when it came time for your broadcast I slipped in the living room and turned up the volume, real high, and came back to play with Rachel.

"You remember her, Daddy. Her father was killed last year in that automobile wreck on Route 3. I was afraid if I told her I wanted to go inside and see my daddy on television it would remind her of her father and make her sad. So I turned you on and listened. I'm sorry if that makes you mad."

Your reasoning and reason were accepted. I was no longer upset at being ignored. I was not mad. Instead I was very glad that my daughter had shown such consideration for a friend. It was I who should have said 'I'm sorry,' but even that would not have let me feel less like a cad. You made me proud.

You Keep the Check

The first thing I ever asked Jack Nicklaus to do he vehemently refused.

He was the newest "phenom" on the PGA Tour, armed with an assortment of titles, including the U.S. Amateur and NCAA and a victory over the professionals in the Ohio Open.

When he turned pro it was as though another era of golf was about to begin. And did it ever!

Much was expected of the Buckeye Basher but his start had been modest. His first professional check was for less than $20. That is his prize check, not counting endorsements. If it was a learning experience, he proved to be a fast learner.

The week before the 1962 U.S. Open at Oakmont the tourists came to Upper Montclair CC in New Jersey, my home club. It was the first really big-money purse in the East, sponsored by auto dealers and known as the Thunderbird Classic.

It was a super-colossal invitational event, organized by the master showman, Fred Corcoran. Every former winner of a major championship was invited. Some had not competed in years. As the drafted chairman of the Press committee, I had written to each at their last known address – and to make it easy for them to reply, a self-addressed, stamped postal card was included. Almost all of these aged and aging former champions responded.

For some their PGA, Open and Masters victories had been decades before and maybe that was why, surprised by an invitation to compete again, they signed their cards but declined.

The reply cards were saved and these autographs from an earlier era I preserved. They read like a "Who's Who" of all the greats of the two decades before. Legends all.

Nicklaus was not yet a legend but he was spoken of as a future legend and his entry pleased the sponsors.

He played well if not spectacularly. Being near the top he was definitely in contention the final round. Another few birdies might erase the "non-winner" identification from his PGA biographical record sheet.

Nicklaus birdied the long 18th hole and became the "leader in the clubhouse." The vast Metropolitan press contingent was impressed. As he climbed toward the top they thought this might be his first professional victory, one week before the Open. It would make quite a story.

Gene Littler came in later, also birdied the 18th and won by a couple strokes, dropping Jack into second place.

The Thunderbird Dealers had the conventional oversized check for the huge sum of $25,000 to present to the winner. They also had prepared a check for the runner-up. It was of a non-conventional size and the amount was $10,000.

With photographers still shooting Littler and the auto dealers and the big check, a dejected Nicklaus quietly retreated to the locker room. He thought his day's work was done.

In the press tent, which had been erected over the parking lot, next to the locker room, several reporters asked if I was bringing Jack into the interview area while they waited for Littler.He had not won but this, by far, was his best showing to date on the PGA Tour. Back to the locker room I went. Jack sat on a bench, all alone, taking off his spikes. On the bench beside him lay the prop $10,000 check.

"Jack, the press would like to talk with you about that fine charge you put on today. May I take you out to the Press tent?"

He looked intently at me for a moment and said he'd prefer not to go. Actually, he refused.

"Lincoln Werden from The Times and several others really want to talk with you," I pleaded. "It won't take long but I surely would appreciate it if you'd come with me."

"They don't want to talk with me," Jack said. "I didn't win. They just need to talk with Littler."

"You finished second," I reminded him, "and they would like your reaction to being in a position to win and almost winning."

It was those last two words that triggered his Teutonic retort. He picked up the $10,000 check and tossed it toward me. It fell quietly to the floor. And then he said something that should have foretold me here was a different kind of hero.

As the check lay on the floor between us he said, "I didn't come out here to win checks. I came out here to win tournaments. You can have the check (it was non-negotiable). If you don't win the tournament, you don't win. I didn't win."

There was the Nicklaus creed in a nutshell. He carried that desire to win tournaments – not checks for finishing second or third or whatever – throughout his career. His determination for victory never waned – not on the regular tour, Senior tour, Skins games or any other endeavor.

Oh, yes. He did relent and let me take him to the Press tent for the interview. It was short but productive and one could sense Jack didn't particularly enjoy the experience.

A week later at Oakmont, where he dethroned but did not replace America's golfing hero, Arnold Palmer, Jack felt he belonged in the Press room. He went gladly for the first of many times as the victor of a major championship.

That day he won. Eight days earlier, in a nearly empty locker room at Upper Montclair he had let me know what his golf goals were. He was on his way, greatness lay ahead. Even he could not have known how great.

P.S. I wish I'd kept that fake $10,000 check he tossed toward me.

When a golfer reaches the very top rung of his or her game the competition is so keen that most major championships are decided by one shot, one hole. It may be a drive or it may be a putt, but less often is it a second shot. In match play the second shot is more important than in stroke play, it seems.

Estelle Lawson Page was the first really great golfer I knew. She was known to the press as the "Chapel Hill housewife," having grown up in the home of the University of North Carolina, where Dr. Robert Lawson, her father, was the athletic trainer and team physician for all Tar Heel athletes.

Mostly self-taught, Estelle practiced on a short course near her home. The course had an abundance of par three holes, some fairly long but others quite short. Estelle zeroed in on all of them and scored something like 73 holes-in-one in her career there and elsewhere.

When she was preparing for a national major competition, she took her clubs to Greensboro and practiced at Sedgefield CC, where she maintained a membership. Sedgefield held membership in the USGA and in those days competitors had to belong to USGA-affiliated clubs.

The Sedgefield course offered Estelle so many different type shots she felt a few days practice there would tune up her game for any challenging shot...all except one, perhaps.

It was there she practiced in 1937 before going to Memphis where she defeated Patty Berg, 7 & 6, to win the USGA crown.

Now, about that one exception shot, here's the one:

Estelle was competing in the Southern Amateur at another Tennessee course and all of the dozen outstanding lady players in the country were entered. Almost the same field as the USGA.

The first few matches came her way rather easily until she eventually had a close but winning semi-final, taking it by a 3 & 2 margin, birdies on two of the last four holes.

In the finals she would face a great Kentucky golfer, Marian Miley. Miss Miley was the daughter of a professional and a few years later was murdered during a robbery at the club where her father was employed. But on this day she posed a formidable threat to Page's pursuit of the Southern title.

Estelle respected Marian's ability. She was a long hitter, had a better than average short game and was a deadly putter. If she was to win, Estelle knew she would have to be competitive on every hole. It would be that tough.

The third hole was slightly less than 400 yards, down into a flat valley but then the second shot would need to go sharply uphill to a plateau green, almost surrounded by bunkers. It was not an easy shot, requiring distance, height and brakes.

Estelle in her earlier matches had not once won the hole, halving it three times and losing it once. A good drive meant the second shot would call for a high, soft No. 3 iron in order to get there and stay on.

After her semi-final win, the North Carolina golfer called her caddie aside and told him to meet her at the practice tee at 7 o'clock the next morning. The finals were scheduled for 36 holes, beginning at 8 o'clock.

"I want to get here in time for extra practice with my No. 3 iron," she told him. "I will need that club at the third hole. It has given me trouble all week and I can't afford to give away that hole tomorrow."

The caddie agreed to be ready.

At 7 they began the warm-up, first with her wedge and on up to the No. 3 iron.

Now Estelle really concentrated. The shot must be high, long enough but land softly... a challenge for any one. Until she was satisfied she continued with the iron.

Then it was to the first tee where about 90-100 ladies and 7 men came to watch. The first two holes were halved with pars and a confident Estelle placed her next tee shot in the center of the fairway. So did Miley.

The caddie sat down the bag and already had his hand on the No. 3 iron when Estelle arrived at the ball. One practice swing and then Estelle struck the ball. It rose, as she planned, and headed for the green, looking like a duplicate of the 20 or more she had drilled off the practice tee.

Miley's second also soared toward the raised island green. It could be seen taking a low bounce but appeared to be 12-15 feet to the right of the flagstick.

The two golfers, good friends after years of competition, walked ahead of the gallery and up the incline to the putting surface.

Alas, only one ball was on the green.

It was Miley's.

Across the green walked Estelle and her caddie, him standing better than six feet tall and Estelle just a bit over five. They looked below and there on the sand lay the other ball.

The caddie shrugged his shoulders as he handed her the sand wedge. Then in a sorrowful voice, soft, sincere and personal...just loud enough to be heard by the cluster of on-lookers, the dejected caddie was heard to say:

"Lawsy, Miz Page, for all the good it done us, we might just as well have stayed in bed this morning."

The World Series of 1950 was not a particularly noteworthy series as World Series go, but for me it offered a unique opportunity to serve as a designated go-between working with two titans of their professions.

After the Dodgers lost their bid to overtake the Philadelphia Phillies, Edward R. Murrow had the inspired introspection to invite Brooklyn's Branch Rickey to be an onsite commentator on his CBS Amoco news radio program.

Mr. Rickey, who shared America's great admiration for Murrow, agreed. He would bring to the Murrow show his grandstand observations, elevating the game of baseball to national newsworthy importance.

When the first two games were played in Yankee Stadium, Murrow asked me to help. I was to engage a limousine, sit with Mr. Rickey in his front row box and then escort him to the limo and race downtown to the CBS studios. That part was easy.

The tough part would be when the Series moved to Philadelphia. New logistics. Murrow devised a plan. I was to rent a hotel room and when the game ended I would bring Mr. Rickey to the quiet of that room and play the role of Murrow in an interview.

Mr. Rickey would tell me the subjects about

which he would like to comment. Together we'd frame the questions. The whole exchange would be piped up to New York to be recorded. One of the staff would copy off my questions, type them on cards and at airtime Murrow would voice my words and they would follow with Mr. Rickey's reply.

The first question was short and when Mr. Rickey responded he looked directly at me with his intense sparkling eyes that seemed to be coming from a cave as they peered from under his long and bushy eyebrows. He started: "Well, John, we saw..."

Stop.

Reaching for my notebook, I turned it over and quickly wrote in big bold letters... "Well, ED..."

After each question I flashed the notebook in front of me, so he would remember that on the broadcast it would be Murrow's question to which he responded.

New York got the questions right, blended Mr. Rickey's answers in perfectly and it was a smooth interview.

As assignments go this one was unique and enjoyable but I might have forgotten it except for Mr. Rickey's summation to the ineptitude of the Phillies, who lost all four games.

The last question had dealt with the chances of Philadelphia coming back after losing the first three games. His reply went something like this: "Of course they may but I don't think they will. The team seems cloaked in indifferences as though they are dazzled by the Yankee brilliance.

"As an example look at what happened on Seminick's last appearance today. With a man on second he sent a weak grounder toward shortstop. Two men were out and this should have ended the inning. The Philadelphia catcher took only three or four casual steps toward first on what he suspected was a futile trip. But the ball was booted, rolled to short left field.

"Lo, wherefore art thou, Seminick? He had become a spectator.

"He had committed a cardinal sin of athletic contests, which is...'Never concede perfection to the opposition."

Mr. Rickey was looking directly into my eyes, although he was talking about Andy Seminick. I've never forgotten his statement or his look About 15 times a round I recall his statement:

"Never concede perfection to the opposition."

I wait for my worthy golfing opponents to three-putt. I wait. And I wait...

Mr. Rickey was right...sometimes they do.

Beg Your Pardon, Sir

Knowing or even seeing the President of the United States, in person, used to be a newsworthy experience. With the advent of television and the daily invasion of our homes by office holders and office seekers the aura of our leaders has dimmed.

Nevertheless a question often asked of me when I reminisce about my lifetime experiences and the people I've known, someone in the group asks: "Did you ever run into any presidents?"

The answer is ... only one... but he survived.

When stationed with the 89th Fighter Squadron at Mitchell Field in the early days of World War II, through the good graces of the wealthy mother of my soldier buddy, we were entertained one weekend a month at the Waldorf-Astoria Hotel. It did a lot for our morale to escape to Manhattan for a couple of days.

One Sunday morning I had gone to the Waldorf newsstand and purchased The New York Times. Even with newsprint shortage The Times was voluminous....many sections, many pages. In an effort to extract the sports section, I was wrestling with the paper when I turned the corner by the bank of elevators.

Approaching from the other side of the corner, having bought his Times, was a guest I did not see because of juggling the slipping sections. He had his paper up and didn't see me either.

At the corner we collided, more paper to paper than man to man, but it was sufficient to cause both big Times to fall and scatter on the lobby floor.

I bent down to pick up the papers, feeling it may have been my fault. He bent down also and like a Mack Sennett comedy, his head bumped my head and we both dropped the papers again.

With the air full of apologies, we again retrieved the papers and this time I moved to the side so I could get his paper, straighten out the sections and hand to him.

Until then I had not really looked at the person with whom I had collided. Now as I retrieved the sections, for the first time I actually looked at the gentleman who clutched in one hand those sections that had not fallen and with his other hand seemed to be rubbing his bumped head.

He was immediately recognizable.

All I could say after almost making the 31st President of the United States a casualty of the war was: "I'm sorry, Mr. Hoover."

Faster than the fastest jets, during WWII rumors and scuttlebutt moved from continent to continent, war zone to war zone in an amazing network of incidental intelligence. Never mind the speed of sound or the super sonic spy planes, wagging tongues knew no boundaries, no limitations.

The day Dixie Tighe, war correspondent for International News Service, arrived in New Delhi, she dashed to our CBI Roundup office in Headquarters building. I had never heard of her but she came in and asked by name to see me.

I was not in my office that afternoon.

Early the next day she returned.

Without so much as a warm-up conversation to ask 'how are you' or 'I'm glad to meet you', Dixie exploded with her flow of words – fast, hard words like she wanted to appear tough.

"I heard in Italy you are a friend of Mahatma Gandhi," she asserted. "Is that true?"

I confirmed that through the courtesy of his son I did know Mr. Gandhi, but it would be presumptive to say I was his friend, more like a comfortable acquaintance.

That's what I told her. In my own mind I knew I could call him my friend.

"As you probably know, Mr. Gandhi has not given an interview during the war. No one can get to him. Since you know him, I'd like for you to arrange an interview for me."

That would not be possible I told her. Simply because I know and visit him occasionally I would not attempt to change his policy.

"I was told in Europe you could arrange it."

Someone told you wrong.

"If I could have just five minutes, just five minutes with him, I could write a favorable story for INS that would be front page news around the world."

Impossible.

"You could come with me and I promise to take no more than five minutes of his time." She was persistent.

Then Dixie asked how long I had been in India.

"I imagine it's quite lonely for a young single man like you. If you can get me that interview with Gandhi, I'm prepared to do anything for you."

A crinkly smile broke out of the corner of her mouth and her eyelids seemed to flutter. She repeated the offer and this time she seemed to underline the word "anything."

That sounded like a barter. Maybe she wanted to send me some pipe tobacco from home or maybe put my name in her story.

Well, I can ask him, I thought, but I know the answer.

That afternoon I biked out to Gandhi's home. He lived in a very plain Indian dwelling, near the outskirts of New Delhi, about four and a half miles from my office but that was no trip on my bicycle. On the way there I pondered in my mind if I really should try to persuade this great Indian leader to do the interview.

I had met Gandhi through his son, Devadas, a newspaper reporter in the print shop where we published the CBI Roundup, our Theater newspaper. I had been welcomed under the Gandhi roof as a friend of his son...not as an American soldier or a reporter, but as a true trusted friend of the youngest Gandhi son. Was I in danger of disturbing that friendship and trust?

As was often the case when I came there, Gandhi was seated on the floor in his living room (which served as an office, a snack room and a nap room).

Afraid I would lose my nerve, I went straight to the purpose of my unexpected visit. I told him an old newspaper friend of mine from New York was in town and had asked me to see if she could have a very brief meeting with him. She would like five minutes and I would be with her to keep it short.

He was silent, as he often was, but seemed to be giving serious consideration. I had expected a quick refusal.

"If she is a friend of yours I can give her five minutes, but no more."

At 4:15 we arrived by cab and went straight into the room where Gandhi sat on the floor, writing as usual with a quill pen.

I introduced demurely-dressed Dixie, less glamorous now than she had seemed at our first meeting and older than I thought. Yes, definitely older.

She hit the ground running. Without a pause she began... "Mr. Gandhi, I am so delighted to meet you. I have known of your fight to bring freedom to India and what you are doing is wonderful. There is so much of interest in your life that I could never begin to do a proper interview in five minutes."

She paused to breathe. I was keeping time on my watch but I had not noticed that Gandhi, upon our arrival, had moved the big round, silver-colored Ingersoll pocket watch – the kind they sometimes call a turnip – over in front of him.

He picked up the watch and when she paused, he spoke for the first time. His words were... "You've wasted 40 seconds already."

At the four minute mark – on my watch – I lightly placed my hand on her shoulder and suggested only one more question. She ignored that, too.

At five minutes, I spoke up, thanked Mr. Gandhi, took her arm and began to walk toward the door. Still she hung back for just one more question.

At seven minutes we re-entered the waiting cab and she dropped me off at my office while she went on to her hotel to write her world-wide scoop interview.

Surprising me, the next day she flew to China, developed an Asiatic fever and died there.

It turned out every one "wasted 40 seconds."

One spring day when I was 10 years old I came home from school and walked up the 300-foot red clay hill road to my home. We had two roads, both unpaved. The hill road was shorter and we used that in good weather. The long road was nearly level but much longer. Even in bad weather it was usable, no slipping or sliding and very little chance of getting stuck in mud. But when I came from school, hungry and in a hurry, I usually used the shorter, steeper hill road.

On this day as I came up the road, lugging my books, I saw my father sitting on the windswept corner of the porch that wrapped its way around three sides of the house. I saw three men sitting and talking with him.

As was expected of me when I got to the top of the hill I continued on toward the side yard and rear of the house. That was where the kitchen was, where the food I craved was waiting for me. This was more important than Daddy's guests.

Before I got by the corner, my father called for me to come up on the porch. This was unusual for as a general rule we were trained not to barge in where adults were talking.

"I want you to meet these gentlemen," he said, as I shyly approached, still clutching my school books.

"These are some very distinguished

gentlemen. This is my son. Shake hands with Mr. Henry Ford, Mr. Harvey Firestone and Mr. Thomas A. Edison."

Each warmly extended his hand and probably made the little small talk one would expect when a father introduces his son.

"You can run along now. I know you're hungry." He was right. I excused myself and headed for the kitchen. I had met my father's visitors but was unimpressed. Since Daddy drove a Ford car I was familiar with that name and thought I had seen his face. My mother explained who the others were.

Friends with whom I've shared this experience always ask what these giants of commerce wanted from my father. The explanation is simple. They wanted information and evaluations.

My father was a well-traveled, self-educated man. He read a great deal and I thought he knew more about more interesting subjects than anyone I ever met. His curiosity for knowledge was well known in our area. People were aware of this trait.

He instilled that desire to learn in all his children. From early childhood, when our vocabularies were limited, each of us was expected to read each issue of the National Geographic and be able to answer his questions about what we had read. When we encountered words we did not know or comprehend there was the ever present dictionary to solve the mystery.

These men had questions for my father that the dictionary did not answer.

Mr. Ford had heard that cottonseed oil, a by-product of the cotton farmers in the South might have an additional use in the preparation of a lubricant for automobiles. Research by his chemists had encouraged Mr. Ford to search for the answer and someone told him Daddy would know. The viscosity of the oil was heavier (or lighter, I can't remember which) than the oil then on the market and might have commercial value.

Mr. Ford came to see Daddy to learn more about the oil.

Mr. Firestone, of course, was manufacturing automobile tires. This was before the development of steel belted tires and cotton cord was used in the manufacture. The best, safest and most durable tires used cord made from long staple Egyptian cotton, which had to be imported at an expensive cost.

Daddy was aware that farmers in our area had been experimenting with different strands of cotton, seeking something that might match the Egyptian variety. If successful it would open up a new market for Southern farmers and be cheaper for the tire manufacturers.

Mr. Firestone came to learn first hand of these experiments.

What about Mr. Edison, oldest of the trio? It seems that he was "bumming" a ride back to New Jersey. In Florida, Mr. Edison lived next door to

Mr. Firestone and had been invited to ride along with the others as they drove north.

Daddy wasn't able to help Mr. Edison, but Mr. Edison could have helped us. At the time we were still using kerosene lamps to light our home. Electricity came two years later when Daddy purchased a Delco battery system. It had about 24 huge, gurgling batteries that had to be regularly monitored and kept filled with water. That was my job.

Eventually the lines of the REA (Rural Electrification Authority) reached our farm and brought cheap electricity to us and our neighbors. Our benefactor was sitting there on the porch, not really appreciated by me at the time for being such an influence on the future of the world. That day he was just listening, while his buddies sought answers.

Together with Mr. Edison, Harvey Firestone and Henry Ford spent more than an hour sitting on my front porch, talking and joking with my father, who was not only knowledgeable, but an entertaining conversationalist. It was long ago but that 10-year-old schoolboy still remembers the pats on the head from three men who were truly wise men of industry.

P.S. If only I'd thought to get their autographs.

Before the war when we both lived in Greensboro, Johnny Bulla, and I saw a great deal of each other. There was very little golf, because I enjoyed more just watching him practice. A joy to watch, smooth like molasses. From his home in Virginia, Sam Snead came down often. They had met at a Louisville tournament in 1935 and established a friendship that lasted their lifetimes.

Some of the greatest golf shots I ever saw were engineered by these two lads when they teamed together to play against Clayton Heafner and little Al Smith from Danville. If Snead drove first and stayed in the fairway, this meant Bulla could turn on his after-burner and smoke it. And if you thought Sevvy was good escaping from horrible locations, Bulla was better.

Snead was 23 and Bulla 21, a couple of long hitting young dudes -- that's what they were in the late 30's. They looked for greener pastures. By now a few tournaments were offering as much as $2,000 purses. They pooled their resources and purchased a used car which they hoped would take them to those golden golf riches in California.

Frugal Sam suggested they pool their expenses as well as their winnings. Bulla demurred. Split the expenses but keep your own cash. Bulla won about $1,000 that winter. His Virginia pal smiled as he deposited something over

180

$10,000. Bad choice.

Bulla would enjoy 1941 better. That year he won the Los Angeles Open and $3,500, the year's largest purse on the West Coast. No splitting. Lightly regarded, if at all, before hand, Johnny during the second round at Riviera posted seven consecutive 3's. He led after 36 but the next day he played someone else's ball and was penalized two strokes. A final round 69 brought him his first big PGA victory. And a rich one.

He finished second in the British Open in 1939, edged out by a birdie on the 72nd hole. The lanky long-hitting pro might have won the British Open in 1946 if he had not been such a persuasive salesman.

Bulla was living in Chicago, where he became a nightly attraction at a local driving range, sending the ball deep into the night, straight and true. Among those who heard of his prowess was Charles Walgreen, the drugstore guru. Walgreen featured a couple of low cost golf balls, the Po-Do, selling for $.25 and named for Charlie's dog, and the Golden Crown at $.45. They needed a golfer to endorse and promote them. Bulla's ability to hit a low-priced drugstore ball clear out of sight earned him the job.

Boo-Boo, as he was called, wanted to go back and play in the British Open again. He had come so close. Walgreen heard his plea and agreed to underwrite his try in 1946. Bulla asked his buddy, Snead, to go with him. Sam thought the

British Open was a bad gamble. It cost too much, it paid too little. Bulla plotted to meet with Sam's boss at Wilson, a gentleman named L.B.Icely, and to tell him Sam was anxious to play at St. Andrews, but felt it was too costly. Naturally Wilson wanted Sam's exposure just as Walgreen did with Bulla. Snead got a free ride to the British Open, thanks to Johnny.

Who knows? That persuasion may have cost Bulla his only major victory. Both played St. Andrews well and were tied for the 54-hole lead at 215. The next day both should have 'called in sick.' Snead scored 75 but Bulla signed for 79, egad. Even so Johnny tied with defending Bobby Locke in second place at 294.

Only the reluctant Snead had beaten him.

An aside in that final round. A New York sportswriter, Richards Vidmer, a big Snead fan, called to Sam's attention as he left the Road hole at 17, the winning ball from each Open is placed on display in the R & A clubhouse. He suggested to Sam that perhaps he should play a Wilson ball on the last hole instead of the brand he had used for 71 holes. He changed.

You need to be careful about such things, y'know.

Bulla was always inquisitive, and a good thinker. He was good enough to be a professional hypnotist. Reincarnation was of special interest and he studied with Edgar Cayce. John Reuter, who designed the Bull's Eye putter, often asked Bulla to evaluate his new projects. At his own expense, Johnny took flying lessons, earned his commercial license and piloted Eastern Airlines schedules between Miami and Chicago during WW11. His L.A. victory so pleased Mr. Walgreen that he gifted him with a four-place Stinson Detroiter.

Bulla may have been the first PGA professional to commute to tournaments in his own plane and he paid for the gas by inviting a few pro friends to go along. Ahead of his time. He later formed a regional aviation company, Arizona Airways. And designed half a dozen good golf courses around Phoenix, where he was an icon.

He had some misadventures in the air but they are not always the pilot's fault. I recall that in 1942, flying from Greensboro to Pinehurst, we flew over an area where the U.S. Army was staging its war games. Bulla was going to play in a pro-am. When we landed at Pinehurst, four MPs in full battle regalia dashed up to our plane, ordered us out, hands up and revealed that we were "prisoners of war" for the duration of the war games.

Some alert anti-aircraft lad had zeroed in on us, somewhere near Goldston. He claimed a hit. So we were dead. The MPs tagged Bulla, his shoes and his clubs. My shoes and my typewriter also were marked as enemy contraband. Dead.... casualties of war. Of course, Bulla regained his clubs and finished second in the Pinehurst tournament.

Back in Greensboro a few days later, Bulla and I saw my managing editor at Starmount Forest Country club. Instead of offering congratulations to Bulla on his high finish, he asked "What do you mean letting us get scooped on your trip to Pinehurst?"

Neither of us understood the challenge. Every day the results had been reported in the paper, especially when a home town boy was among the leaders. We sought an explanation.

"Yesterday's New York Times printed an AP item that was headed:
GOLF PRO, WRITER
WAR GAMES VICTIMS
The story stated you were shot down and victims in the Army War Games. And we didn't have a word on it in our paper. "

I told you Bulla was a thinker. He turned to my editor and asked....." How could we? It said we were dead."

Until his death in the winter of 2003, Bulla was busy with golf, airplanes and family and family came first. He loved Phoenix and was always concerned that one day an eruption might slide half of California into the Pacific Ocean. Arizona was close enough.

For a golf professional who was only two putts away from victory in two British Opens and who played well in seven others; a man who finished as high as second at Augusta, was

184

invited and played there 15 times; and a man who competed in 18 USGA Opens and had 12 top 10 finishes in the Majors, it's hard to call him just another run of the fairways golf professional. He wasn't. He was a leader, a teacher and a man to be admired.

Bulla was a natural....but was it left or right? He competed from the right but could play equally as well from the left. He once finished second in the National Lefthanders tourney. He could beat you either way. You choose.

Still appreciated in his native area, Bulla was voted into the Carolinas Golf Reporters Hall of Fame. As a member I was pleased to be asked to deliver the induction. I agreed.

Three days later, a letter from Bulla said he had heard the news of his new honor. He was thrilled, but confided he was not well enough to attend. As an old friend, he asked if I would stand in for him, thank the hosts and accept the trophy. I agreed.

It was unusual to give and receive the same trophy, but I did. Left hand to give. Right hand to receive. Both for Boo-Boo.

It was nearly mid-afternoon Paris time and I had just come from an exhilarating experience. I had addressed the Anglo-French Press Club. Never before had I given a talk where my remarks had to be made in short takes and then I had to wait for the French translation. One gets the unique feeling of elongated lapses of thought. Your mind reacts like an automobile direction signal... left....right....stop....go....yes...no....

As we strolled along the Rue de Curison with David Schoenburn, the CBS bureau chief, en route to his office he said the talk had been well received. Everything seemed so upbeat and happy.

When we arrived at the CBS office, we learned Ed Murrow wanted me to call him in New York. It was not unusual for Murrow to call Schoenbrun as Dave's reports were heard almost nightly on Murrow's news program. It was morning in New York but Murrow had tracked me down in Paris and wanted me to call him.

The date: August 16, 1948.

"Babe Ruth is dead," Murrow said. "He had cancer, as you know. I'd like for you to do a personal eulogy, a fan's view. We'll tape it when you are ready."

"Give me two minutes on what Ruth meant to you. To have known him at long distance in your youth and then to have had the thrill of getting to know him in person in his last years."

There were no record books available to spur my memory. I could not look up his biography to learn when he was born. I knew it was in Baltimore but little more. To those of us of that era, the 1920's – 1940's, he was our ageless legend, ours.

For a few minutes I sat and recalled to myself how, as a schoolboy in North Carolina, the first thing I looked for each morning in The Charlotte Observer was the sports page.

What did Ruth do yesterday? He didn't hit a home run every day. He didn't? Then I felt disappointed. On his way to his record-setting 60, I remembered my inner joy and satisfaction every time the box scores recorded another homer.

There was no television and little radio, except at World Series time. We had to read about Ruth, look at the newspaper pictures and imagine the sound of his bat on the ball. Then occasionally we'd catch a glimpse of him in the Fox Movietone newsreel. Those spindly legs, big shoulders, ample stomach.

Mostly we created our own aura of this great baseball star. We could believe we heard the crack of the bat and could imagine him tossing it aside as he waddled to first and second and third and home. Our make-believe memory book of Babe Ruth was full of his fantastic exploits and all my friends felt the same.

Seeing Ruth in person was unthinkable at

that time.

I remembered this now, sitting in our Paris office. Years flashed by and I recalled the day Red Barber introduced me to The Babe. Time had not been kind to Ruth and his glory days were past, but he was still an imposing figure of a man.

Barber hosted an early evening radio program for which I was the writer and producer. Ruth was a guest maybe eight or ten times. He would arrive by taxicab at the CBS building early, usually 30 minutes before broadcast time. It was my job to wait for his cab.

In the fall and winter he would be wearing a very long mauve camel-hair coat. This was his trademark coat and helped fans recognize him. He'd sign autographs and then I took him to a reserved elevator to whisk him to the 17th floor.

Those minutes before airtime, while Barber was putting together the final elements of his broadcast, gave me the opportunity to sit and talk with The Babe. He was a smart man. Some folks figured he was a big dumb, brainless athlete. Not so. He knew a lot more than how to hit a baseball. He may not have been a Rhodes scholar but he was a kind, considerate conversationalist, at least in the eyes of this fan.

In Paris that afternoon, far from Yankee stadium and other fields of his greatness, I wondered what I could say to Murrow's listeners that would not sound trivial and trite. He was so well known, so admired, so honored in his achievements.

I read to Schoenbrun what I had written.

"That's exactly what your report, your eulogy, should be," said Dave. The sports pages will list his records and achievements. They are history and indisputable. Ed wants to know what the significance of his death means to you – and the millions like you – who grew up in pre-war America, NORTH, SOUTH, EAST AND WEST, with Babe Ruth as a great national hero.

This I tried to do. I have no copy of that script but I do recall my excitement about the opportunity to say my piece. There was a certain incongruity about a lad from the South, who admired this Yankee from afar and then in Ruth's declining years had become an acquaintance. Maybe not close enough to call him my friend, but ever thrilled when he called me by name.

From Paris for Ed Murrow and his CBS audience I did my best to pay honest homage and say "good-bye" to The Babe.

P.S. I wish I had seen him hit one home run in person.

Cricket...in an old foot locker is a faded baseball he signed for me. It was not properly wrapped and when last I looked at it the name was barely legible. No one else would know the faded letters identified my first great hero, a lifelong hero.

Don't throw it out.   JD

"PLEASE EXCUSE THE WRITING"

For 26 years my father was a rural mail carrier. Six days a week he traveled some 35 miles of rural roads, traversing the hills and curves as he delivered the mail through the northern part of Gaston County in western North Carolina.

He wore out 21 Model T and Model A Fords on these country roads most of which were paved by the time he retired. Some were rutted and muddy in rainy weather, and some days when he came home his black Ford looked almost red, but he loved his job and the people he served. For many he was their main contact with the outside world.

As a youngster I wanted to ride that route with him one day, to see the folks about whom I'd often heard him talk. Postal regulations denied me that opportunity. No riders with the mail.

I knew where his route ran, but I wanted to see the patrons as they came to their mail boxes to wait for my father and their mail. He had often told me of the enjoyable smiles of happiness when he had letters for them.

And some days there were packages. Many of these people made much use of the catalogs from Sears Roebuck and Montgomery Ward, the two big Chicago mail order merchants. The mail box was their mall.

Perhaps the biggest smiles, Daddy told me,

were from those who received letters from absent children who more or less regularly sent home checks from their jobs in Chicago or Detroit or New York. These were the entitlements of that day and the children were entitled to assist their down home relatives.

One afternoon when we were going some place we traveled over a part of the route he drove every day. As we passed a weather-beaten unpainted but neat little farm house there was a friendly wave from the lady in the yard.

Daddy waved back to her and a smile came over his face but did not shield the respect and appreciation he had for this friend.

"She's an awfully nice person," Daddy said. "She always bakes us a cake at Christmas. She never went to school, can't read and can't write. When she gets a letter from her daughter in Chicago, I always wait for her and read it to her.

"A funny thing happened last week when she got her check from her loving daughter. After I read her the letter and gave her the check and letter she fairly bubbled with thanks – to me for reading and her daughter for sending the letter.

"The next day when I came by here I had no mail for her but she was standing by the road and signaled me to stop. In her hand she had a pencil and a Blue Horse school type tablet."

" 'Mr. Derr, I would like for you to write a note to my daughter and tell her I received the check.' In her hand she still had the envelop so I could address the reply.

"I took the tablet," Daddy told me, "and she told me the two or three paragraphs, adding a comment on the weather and that all of the family was well. Then she said to end it with 'love' and sign her name."

Daddy did as she requested and she bought a two-cent stamp and put it on the envelop. He was about to seal it when she called out, "Wait. I want to add a P.S."

Exactly as she requested, at the bottom of the single page letter, Daddy added her P.S.: "Please excuse the writing."

TWISTING KNOBS

Occasionally on the TV tower at a golf tournament you are given vocal instructions by your director...instructions that are not always what they sound like. Fortunately the director's comments are on closed circuit lines and do not leave the course.

At the first Colgate-Dinah Shore LPGA tournament at Mission Hills, one of these inexplicable situations developed and it provided Dinah with a gig to torment me for years.

Friday afternoon a dry-run rehearsal was scheduled. As usual, my assignment was the 17th. Sometimes, especially on the LPGA events where we were not as familiar with some of the players, an LPGA non-participant would join us to add background information.

On this day a young professional, who had recently been injured in an accident and was unable to compete, joined me at the 17th tower.

David Foster, CEO of Colgate and a great patron of the girls, was very impressed that this girl, although unable to play, had thought enough of Dinah, Colgate, and the tour to come and attend this first Shore tournament. He suggested we hire her, since she knew all the competitors and their styles.

As the rehearsal began the director opened all lines, gave his usual charge to the troops to stay alert and talk less. Then he asked for voice checks around the circuit.

Everything was okay at 15. Okay at 16, levels were good.

Then he asked for my voice check. Okay. He asked Carol (not her name) to say a few words.

She was seated alongside of me. She was silent. There was no response, not even a nod, but it appeared her lips were moving but the director heard nothing. I heard nothing.

The director asked if she had her headphones on. She did.

It was her first time as a TV reporter and even to old hands sometimes the chatter is confusing. I told her to keep talking, perhaps they would hear her. Nothing.

The director asked if her amplifier was turned on. I had no idea and our technician had gone down from the tower to get some tape.

Possibly aware of my own lack of engineering expertise the struggling director gave me instructions.

"The amplifier is that square metal box on the table. It may not be turned on and open. Reach over in front of Carol and twist her knobs."

From all around the course I could hear the gasps.

The line extended from the control truck to

all on-course cameras and announcers...at 15... at 16...at 18. Someone still on the line screamed: "He just told Derr to twist Carol's knobs. What's going on over there at 17?"

Carol had watched as I reached over and opened the amplifier knobs. She saw what I was doing and didn't even flinch. Not a flutter did I see.

Now she could be heard in the control room. I had done my job. I had twisted knobs. Visibly it was not obscene but apparently some who heard it thought so. They spread and enlarged on the word. That was Friday afternoon.

Sunday at lunchtime I passed by the table where Dinah was sitting with Mr. Foster. He motioned for me to join them. There was no frown but no smile when he said, "I hear you were twisting Carol's knobs out on your tower."

"Yes, what's the meaning of this?" smiled Dinah, who was every bit as sweet and sincere as she seemed. As my face reddened like the tomatoes in Dinah's salad, she continued..."I was afraid we might have a sexual harassment charge on our hands..."

That may have been the first time I ever heard the term, "sexual harassment." I learned if you are told to twist the knobs, do it quietly, and hope no one hears.

After that day whenever I saw Miss Shore her greeting was always this question...

"Twisted any good knobs lately?"

"You work your side of the street and I'll work mine," was the answer I got from Arnold Palmer one day when I asked him if he was interested in going up the tower to try his skills as a golf television commentator.

Unfortunately for some professional reporters who were trained to paint pictures with words instead of knowing how to put maximum backspin on a pitch shot, a great many golfers moved to the tower when their golfing skills diminished. And several of them worked at it to become capable.

Palmer had no interest in that "side of the street" so you may have never heard him do play-by-play. One day at Doral I did and it was all bad.

On that Friday a foursome from our TV crew followed rehearsal by playing nine holes on another Doral course, alongside the Blue Monster. There was a token wager and with Jim McArthur as my partner we came to our final hole.

A putt of about 12 feet faced me and it could decide the match.

As we moved toward the green, people were walking beyond, but not until we got out of our carts did we recognize Gary Player and Palmer, each with a couple of clubs, coming from another practice area.

Fun-loving Arnie decided to have some

fun, and I think he may have waited for this opportunity for some time. At any rate, when he recognized us they came to the green.

Arnie turned his putter upside down, making believe it was a microphone, and proceeded to describe the action. He commented on each player's putts, including his opinions as to how they would break or how fast the green was.

When it was my turn to try the 12-footer I suggested he shut up, this putt was for the money.

"You keep talking when I'm putting (which was not true) and I'm going to keep on."

As I squeezed the putter, this is what I was hearing from Palmer puttherhead network: "And now Derr has this breaking downhill putt, with a break at the end. He probably thinks its about 15 feet, a distance that always gives him trouble. If he misses it he'll say it was 20 feet. It's only 12 feet....Oops he had it lined up on the low side."... and on and on.

It cost me $2 but it was worth it to hear the King himself enjoying the fun he was having at my expense, describing my putt. That may have been the only play-by-play Palmer ever did, working my side of the street, but I enjoyed it.

Another Palmer memory happened at Augusta on a Sunday morning. Travelers Insurance was one of the CBS Television sponsors, and although we did not encourage non-workers on the tower, James Byrne, a Travelers executive who had recently damaged a leg in a skiing accident, was allowed to join me topside.

Before being driven down to our tower position at the 15th green, we sat on a bench inside the ropes at the big tree, looking out over the putting green. Players going to practice used the path behind our bench.

From the corner of my eye I saw Palmer coming out the path. He stopped at our bench, laid his hand on my shoulder and passed the pleasantries of the day before he moved on to the practice putting green.

I never turned to face him, he was standing a bit behind me.

As he walked away Mr. Byrne said, "I wish you had introduced me to Palmer. I need his name on a scorecard."

"Excuse me, I would have thought you had met him"

"Oh, I've met him all right but it was a long time ago. I had a hole-in-one playing with him at Atlantic City and I'd like to have his autograph on the card."

"Wait a minute," I said. "You are telling me you had a hole-in-one while playing with Arnold Palmer and you didn't have him sign the card. This man has signed a million cards but here you had a legitimate reason for him to sign it and he didn't. Why did you not have him sign it?"

Byrne said the other players signed but he failed to ask Palmer. "Why not," I insisted.

"To tell you the truth it didn't seem such a big deal at the time. Palmer was a guest playing at my club. He was in the Coast Guard. We both knew I was more important in golf than he was."

"Pray tell, why were you more important? I wondered aloud, showing some surprise at that ridiculous statement.

"I'll have you know...I was the caddie master."

The dormant card was found and sent to Doc Griffen to be sure Palmer saw it and read the note. I suggested he autograph the card for a hole-in-one he saw made 25 years earlier.

Mr. Byrne now has the signatures of all four players, although one was added quite late.

Watch Those Zeroes

The Town House was a favorite "after Masters" eating place in downtown Augusta in the 50's and 60's. Before the stars started renting private homes and having meals prepared there, the Town House used to attract huge crowds and almost always the winner and his party. They usually had a reserved booth.

One Sunday night there was a flurry of excitement when Winnie and Arnie Palmer and friends arrived. They were escorted to their booth with Arnie stopping along the way to accept congratulations.

Palmer had just scored an exciting victory, but someone at my table commented that he didn't look too happy for a man who had just won a major and a check for $20,000.

A few minutes later the manager walked by and Palmer accompanied him back to the front. I thought it must have been a call from the White House to have him interrupt his victory dinner as I saw him pick up the phone.

Shortly he returned. This time he was beaming, almost buoyant. He called to us as he dashed back toward his booth... "We got it back." He added... "He tried to cash it twice but somebody called the club and now they've got it back..."

We thought Palmer had lost his $20,000 winning check. There was no way anyone could expect to cash a Masters check made out to Palmer, especially on Sunday night. Maybe a little check, but not one that big.

What had changed that pained look of

apprehension on Palmer's face to this current gleam of great relief?

It seems that after the ceremony Palmer gave to his wife, Winnie, the legitimate Augusta National check. Being considerate, as always, he asked Winnie to write the check for his caddie. It would be the biggest caddie check she had ever written and the biggest ever paid for carrying the winner's clubs up those Georgia hills.

His reward would be appropriately big -- $1,200.

Amid all the excitement, the hustle and bustle of the presentation and the general bedlam that follows a tournament, Winnie reached in her handbag, pulled out the checkbook, wrote a check and gave it to the caddie.

He quietly looked at the piece of paper, feigning an indifference that belies the excitement of receiving one's wages, no matter how much.

The tournament over but the caddie, low on funds, remembered he had the check. Four blocks from the club there was a beer parlor, where his version of a victory champagne could be bought. When asked if he had funds, he produced the Palmer check...for a partial cashing. He was refused.

No problem, there was another beer stand two blocks away.

Same experience, except this time the clerk asked if he had found the check. This insulted the caddie and he took his check and continued his quest for a beer.

Not so fast, thought this clerk. He called the club.

"A caddie came in my store and tried to buy some beers with a very large check he said he had been given by Arnold Palmer. I didn't cash it. I couldn't. It was too big. But I thought you might want to check with Palmer to see if there's some mistake."

The club tracked down Palmer and told him the facts.

It was this news that had Arnie looking so perplexed as he and his party first came into the restaurant.

Word went out to find the caddie. The check was recovered. This was the news the club called the Town House to tell Palmer.

Relief? Oops. The check was for $12,000.

How Did I Do It?

An example of great international diplomacy occurred late one afternoon after a round of golf at the Royal Delhi Gymkhana Club. And I still laugh at it.

A British colonel, a typical foreign service Lancashireman, and I had just completed our play. He lived for his golf, his toddy and the Empire, in that order.

As we relaxed on the terrace, watching families of monkeys in single file crossing the first fairway, the colonel remembered he had played the past weekend in a club tournament.

He rang the signal cord for the steward. The dignified Indian gentleman, frocked completely in white except for the brilliant blue sash and his decorated turban, answered the call.

"Have they completed the Swinburne competition, steward?"

"Yes, sir."

"And how did I finish?"

With unrestrained enthusiasm, the steward fairly bubbled as he proudly replied, "You were second, sir."

"Jolly good," beamed the colonel, looking to see if I had been properly impressed by his high finish in the Swinburne.

"And how many were in the competition?"

"Two, sir."

"Oh, I see," responded the somewhat crestfallen colonel, but as if to assure himself that second really wasn't all bad, he drained the last of his toddy, looked blankly off into space for a couple of moments, then turned to me and repeated the news he'd learned from the diplomatic steward. "Well, I was second, you see."

Yes, I thought but did not say, you were also last.

Still Looking, Sahib?

When Gen. Sir Archibald Wavell, Viceroy of India, played at the Delhi Club he was always accompanied by a retinue of white-uniformed caddies, in addition to the tall Indian boy who was chief caddie. He carried the clubs. I think his wartime assignment was custodian of the Viceregal clubs.

One day on a dogleg hole on the back nine, my foursome of fellow GIs, plus regular and two extra caddies inexplicably lost a ball. We fanned out to search through the scrubby bushes but saw nothing of the lost ball. In those days balls were hard to find and even used balls were most expensive so the six caddies and our four GIs searched quite some time.

One of our caddies noticed the approach of Viceroy Wavell and his group so we did as expected. We stopped all motion of looking for the ball, waved them through and stood respectfully quiet a proper distance off the fairway. This was protocol when players noticed the Super Rajah approaching.

He courteously acknowledged our standing by and waved greetings as his procession marched on. We resumed our search.

The next day, our other day off that week, my friends and I returned to the golf club to resume our play. This day we had almost as big a platoon as the Viceroy normally had. There the four Yanks, four caddies and we had hired four fore-caddies in hopes of not losing any more balls. And, oh yes, the caddies had a few friends who were unpaid ball hawks who hoped to find a "lost" ball and be handsomely rewarded for their diligence.

Would you believe when we reached that same hole, the one that bent right in a sharp dogleg, we had another lost ball. Once more our little platoon took to the rough and searched.

Speaking of déjà vu, almost on cue someone looked back and yelled, "Here comes the Viceroy." The platoon approached.

Again we signaled for them to proceed and again we stood by, not to resume our search until they had played through. Once more the Viceroy came near our side of the fairway and expressed his appreciation.

As he moved away I could almost swear I heard him say to one of his companions: "Can you believe they are still here?"

Soon after my arrival at Karachi, India, as a member of the 89th Fighter Squadron, USAF, in an irregular requisition, I was transferred to the personal staff of the China-Burma-India Theater commander, Lt.-Gen. Joseph W. Stilwell.

It was several weeks after I reached New Delhi before I actually saw the recognizable figure of Stilwell. Wearing circular wire-framed glasses and with his butch haircut showing traces of gray he looked exactly like his pictures, the pictures that showed him marching out of Burma to escape the Japanese.

One point needs clarification here. There are those who refer to this military leader as "Vinegar Joe" Stilwell. To those of us who really knew him, he was "Uncle Joe." Forget the vinegar. That misnomer has always been repugnant.

Stilwell had been in Burma in what the troops called the "weeds." He preferred it out there – with his troops.

The clean sheets and marble staircases of New Delhi he left to others. He'd as soon pitch his tent in the jungle. He looked upon headquarters assignments as "clerical duty" and, showing his disdain for the typewriter brigade he was heard to say... "No Underwood ever killed an enemy..."

When he was in New Delhi, Stilwell was quite visible around the low-slung one-story stucco headquarters building. He went to his office almost every night, usually alone. I don't know what he was working on but he may have been doing as many of us did, while away an Indian evening – writing to our families and friends.

Occasionally at night the General would come down the hall to our CBI ROUNDUP office – to relax from war and talk a little sports. There wasn't much USA sports news available in India except in our weekly theater newspaper and my column.

It was on one of these night visits I learned that Stilwell had chaired the committee at West Point that wrote the first codified collegiate basketball rules. Until then every conference played by its own set of rules.

"Do you want to know a strange coincidence?" I asked. "In 1935 I attended a rules seminar conducted by Katherine D. Meyer of NYU at the UNC Women's College in Greensboro, N.C. Until then there had been no universal rules to govern women's basketball. I wasn't chairman but I helped write the first rules for women's basketball. It took three days."

During the war I was fortunate that many friends sent books to me. One night there were new books by my desk and General Stilwell asked if I read many books. I nodded yes.

"I'd like to borrow this one, after you've read it," the General said and I urged him to take it then as I had the other two which I hadn't read.

"I'll take this one and send you one you may enjoy." He sent me a hardcover blue book, entitled "The Defence of Dover Harbour." (Cricket, that spelling is correct since that is the way the British spell defense).

It had been written by two British military strategists after World War I and there were numerous stick type drawings to show where to line up the mortars and the troops. It was to me a very dull book...no plot, no pictures.

Expecting the General to drop in again some early night I placed his book by my desk, inserted a bookmark after 40 pages to make it look as though I was reading it.

I had given up on page 5.

Sure enough the General noticed the book and asked how I was enjoying it. I lied. But I did move the bookmark over another 75 pages, in case he came by again. I thought if it looked like I had finished the book, I could return it, thank him and forget it.

Wrong.

The next time – a week or so later – he asked my opinion on the defense strategy advocated by the authors. I fumbled and stumbled and felt I had obfuscated enough to get by.

"Sergeant, you haven't read that book."

That was all he said but no teacher, anywhere, ever made me feel more guilty of criminal deception than those six words and the unsmiling look on the general's face.

The bookmark had made it all the way through the book but my knowledge of "The Defence of Dover Harbour" had ended on page 5... very early on.

"Sir, I finished the book but I did not read every page. I found it too hard for me to understand. I'm sorry."

Stilwell silently handed the book back to me.

The fly leaf of the book had been signed by Stilwell as it was his personal book. He told me to return it to him only after I had completely read it.

If they ever attack Dover Harbour I hope somebody who's read it will tell them what to do. If they need the book, I have a very slightly used copy.

Meanwhile there was a World Series coming up. The Cards were winning in the National but three clubs battled for the American flag. A wartime series wouldn't be much but all around the world the American troops would be interested.

Since my Roundup sports column and my weekly broadcast over All-India Radio, the BBC outlet for Asia, were the principal sources of sports news, General Stilwell agreed I should fly home – 17,000 miles – to report the Series for the troops.

Orders were cut, stating I was to visit

continental United States on a mission for the Theater Commander, and upon completion of my mission (no dates given) I would return to my assigned station, which was New Delhi.

Time Magazine called it the longest sports assignment in history...from New Delhi to St. Louis and return.

While I was away, General Stilwell was reassigned and I was not able to return his book... or to read it.

There was an anxious look on the face of the young caddie as he lifted my golf bag from the trunk of my rented car. "Your bag is mashed." He had removed the thin black vinyl travel cover from the bag and laid it beside him. He stood there while I folded up the cover and tossed it in the trunk.

Now to dig for my shoes. There was no time to go to the locker room at the Country Club of Salisbury. Sit on the edge of the trunk and slide into the spikes, even with no shoe horn.

The caddie still stood there, holding the bag on the ground and showing no sign of moving toward the first tee.

"Come on," I said. "The others are already there and we have to get going." He slung it over his shoulder at last.

This is not the preferred way to rush to the first tee, barely getting your shoe laces tied. No warm-up on the range. No practice putts. Maybe in this case that was good for it also meant no time to get nervous.

What was there about this game to make me nervous?

For one thing I could see a gallery of a couple hundred golf fans around the first tee. Some of them, maybe most of them, were better players than this late arrival.

On the tee was the host professional, Gene Thompson, chatting with good-looking Sharon Moran, an all-around good athlete, tennis and golf. She not only possessed a winning game but a winning smile and was generally acclaimed as the prettiest athlete on tour. I had not voted…but I agreed with the decision.

Patiently standing alone, already with driver in hand, flipping it gently back and forth, wearing the white linen cap that was then his trademark, was Byron Nelson.

At this point I should explain why I was in this distinguished company. I was en route to televise the Greater Greensboro Open and had flown to Charlotte, rented a car and driven to Salisbury to attend the National Sportscasters and Sportswriters dinner in that city.

This dinner annually attracts stars from my sports – football, auto racing, baseball, tennis and golf. It was the golf exhibition that interested me – Moran, Nelson, Arnold Palmer and Thompson, the home pro.

When I had driven into the parking lot, minutes before, Thompson saw me get out of the car and called out…" "Where are your clubs?"

"In the trunk. Why?"

"Arnie sent word he won't be able to make it and I want you to take his place in the exhibition."

"You've got to be kidding."

"No. Put on your shoes and let's go."

The gallery had been told Palmer was not going to make it so there were no boos when Thompson explained I had been drafted to complete the foursome. Disappointment but no boos. Nelson was to be my partner.

The first hole was uneventful. I had taken the driver and found the right side of the fairway. I went to my bag and pulled out the No. 6 iron and succeeded in getting on the green. Two putts and I was thrilled to be off so well.

The second hole was longer and I figured my No. 5 wood second might get to the green. I reached for it. When I lifted the club from my bag, the head came loose and the shaft dangled, before falling to the ground.

I was shocked.

The caddie said, "I told you your bag was mashed."

What about the other clubs, I wondered.

We turned up the bag and clubs and parts of clubs came tumbling onto the grass. I knew three clubs were okay – the driver, No. 6 iron and the putter – but the others were a mess.

Both other woods had lost their shafts. The wedge and No. 8 iron were fine. Every other iron was bent or headless.

Nelson came to look and called to Thompson. "There's an oak tree. That's solid. Let's see if we can straighten some of these shafts." Nelson and Thompson went to work.

While I stood helplessly by these two pros got four more irons straight enough to use and we continued the exhibition.

Meanwhile the gallery had become supportively sympathetic, wondering how I could be expected to play with damaged clubs.

When I got over the jolt I became livid. At the Charlotte Airport my golf bag had fallen on the ground and had been run over by these steeled-rimmed wheels of the baggage cart. I had noticed the cover had a tear in it and the caddie had told me the bag was mashed but I hadn't expected this much damage.

Whether it was because my concentration was more focused when trying to play damaged clubs or just plain luck, but I finished the front nine with a respectable 39, four over par.

Earlier I had asked Gene to find a replacement for the replacement and after nine I turned things over to a local member and went to a phone to complain to Eastern Airlines.

When Dick Bailey, president of the network, heard about my misfortune, he told me not to report it to Eastern because Eastern was one of our sponsors.

"We will buy you a new bag and a complete set of clubs, just don't say anything to Eastern," he urged. Too late.

EAL eventually supplied me with a new bag and clubs but I never understood why I had to turn over to them all of the clubs that had been in the bag. The putter was not damaged and it was a favorite of mine.

Although I did a number of telecasts with Nelson, who was one of the really compassionate sports stars, I played only those memorable nine holes with him. This kept him from ever knowing that playing with slightly bent clubs was about as well as I could play with new sticks, but he never forgot.

Nelson retired early and followed his playing and teaching career by moving into the television booth. Despite his outstanding knowledge of the game and the players, there was a time when his commentary did not satisfy the networks or the public. Byron's soft Texas tones were over-shadowed by others whose louder and more forceful exhortations contrasted with his quieter, less dramatic comments.

Nelson was replaced and many of his friends were unhappy with the turn of events. They felt politics ousted him. He had been good, but in broadcasting sometimes good is not enough.

Del Webb, owner of the Sahara Hotel in Las Vegas and former co-owner of the New York Yankees, was a friend of Nelson's who knew how much the shoddy treatment had affected Byron. Webb sponsored the Sahara Invitational tournament in Las Vegas.

One day Webb called me at my home in Center Lovell, ME., and told me he had arranged for his tournament to be televised over a Western regional network.

Webb asked if I would come out and host the telecast. Even though it was only a regional telecast, he would pay me my usual network fee, which was modest – quite modest – in those days.

"The fish are biting up here," I told him, trying to find an excuse for turning down his invitation.

Webb said, "I've arranged for Byron to work with you. I think he got a bum rap on his last television work. I like his reporting and if he is working alongside you I think the public can appreciate how knowledgeable he is. You two would be a great team."

The flattery persuaded me.

At the Friday rehearsal, Nelson and I sat side by side on the tower overlooking the 18th green. I told the west coast producer I wanted a unique setup. I wanted both of our mikes open at all times – an unheard of risk, thought the producer.

"We can't do that," I was told. "We'll open his mike for him to answer your questions, but it is not a good idea to have his mike open all the time."

I insisted. "We are going to talk about the action here as though we are two golf fans, watching at greenside. We will talk back and forth, like fans do. I want both mikes open at all times to be sure our casual conversation is not lost. I will be responsible."

The 18th was a rather shortish par four, sharp dogleg to the right. Long hitters flirted with fading the ball to the top of the hill, leaving a short iron to the banked green. There was wild country inside the dogleg and the sandy, clumpish rough to the left could, result in a difficult lie.

Airtime arrived. Nelson and I were to chat, back and forth, but to start the commentary, I gave an update on earlier play and set the stage for action. Back on the 18th tee the cameras picked up the next group. The first two drives were played to the top of the mounds, in the fairway, safe. The third player, going with his driver, blew it straight away and went through the fairway. There was no grass there, only a few tumbleweeds.

Conversationally I asked Byron why a player would take that longer, dangerous route. It had been about four minutes since the broadcast began and I wanted to get Byron into the flow.

I looked toward him. His lips were moving but no words came out. His throat had dried up. I knew the feeling. I knew the feeling because it had happened to me and every other person unfamiliar with a live mike. But it's not fatal. As though I was interrupting him, I quickly said... "I guess he was trying to fade the ball and instead it came out straight."

That interval did the trick. Byron picked

up the line, confirmed that my uninspired guess was the way it looked to him and for 90 minutes there was never an awkward moment. It was one of the most relaxed, enjoyable and informative golf telecasts I ever did.

At the first commercial break, Nelson thanked me for picking up after that opening question when the words were silent.

I told him to relax. It was my job to get us out of any "unplayable lies." If we were playing the course that would be his job – to rescue me from my inadequacy – but problems in the telecast booth were mine and I'd handle them.

Webb and other friends of Nelson's had been listening in the Paradise Valley CC clubhouse. When Nelson climbed down from the tower they were waiting for him on the ground. It was good to hear him on the broadcast. They knew he had been hurt and vindication was strong medicine.

I never enjoyed the reaction to a broadcast more than seeing the smiles and handshakes by the Nelson friends. He had performed as Webb and I knew he would, given the proper circumstances.

Sunday night at the Sahara there was a reception for the winner, many of the other contestants who stayed around, and special guests of party-giver Webb. It was a joyous loud time.

After about an hour Webb called me aside and we entered the elevator to go from the mezzanine to the lobby. But we never got there. En route Webb punched a button and we stopped between floors. I was later told that this unscheduled stop was a device used often in Las Vegas. The between floors stop was the only place in the hotels that couldn't be bugged.

There was no great need for secrecy. Webb told me Nelson had received many favorable calls from friends and that it had been a successful tonic. "I think he'll now do a lot more telecasts," Webb added. And he did, enjoying a long career as the expert analyst for ABC.

Webb released the button and we returned to the party, but not before he told me... "There'll be a little bonus in my check..."

Nelson's quick recovery "earned" me an extra $2,000 bonus.

The Kentucky Derby was the fiefdom of Col. Matt Winn, a distinguished son of the Blue Grass state, who saw the 1875 Derby as a 14-year-old boy, standing in his father's wagon in the infield. He saw every Derby during his lifetime, most of them while serving as president and major domo of the Derby. He was the Derby and one mustn't ever forget it.

The 1948 running of the Derby would be of special interest to you, Cricket. Colonel Winn invited your mother to sit with him in his box at the finish line. This was the day Citation won the first leg of the Triple Crown. To have been in the company of Colonel Winn, close enough to check the breathing of Citation en route to his glorious triumph thrilled Peggy.

Colonel Winn was a crafty old soul. And once I was matched against him in a high stakes "poker game" that I had to win.

The Kentucky Derby had long been a sports spectacle but with the maws of television demanding more great sports events CBS wanted all broadcast rights to the Derby week action. We had the Belmont in New York and the inside track on getting the Preakness.

NBC had broadcast the Derby a few times and ABC joined in once or twice, but no one had ever paid much for rights. Winn wanted the national publicity. But now he was going to sell the rights. We were notified he was open to bids.

CBS told me to "get the Derby." I dared not fail.

There are few secrets amongst the networks, then or now. NBC knew what ABC would offer and we were in the same range, so something besides money would earn the Derby rights.

A friend of Winn's in Louisville told me the kind of food he liked, so I would know where to take him for dinner in New York.

"Is there anything else about Colonel Winn that I should know that might help me convince him to come with CBS?"

"There's only one other thing," my friend said. "As you know the Colonel is proud of the bands he brings here and he is especially fond of our Kentucky anthem – 'My Old Kentucky Home.' NBC faded out the band after one verse and I don't think the Colonel liked that. He loves to hear that song."

When the Colonel came on his selling trip to New York, each of us entertained him. He liked my dinner choice at D'Avico's. Then we went back to his hotel room for serious talk.

"Colonel, I think I know what money is being offered and we can't go much higher. We'd like to have the Derby, to go with the Belmont and Preakness, but our budget is tight, too. However, if we do get it, there's one change I'd like to make in the schedule.

"My people have given me permission to expand the broadcast by 15 minutes. That's longer than any race anywhere. I want that time so CBS can broadcast all four stanzas of "My Old Kentucky Home.""

The Colonel's face was impassive during most of my talk. As I had heard, he was a great poker player. But as I closed my offer, there was a twinkle in his aging, happy eyes.

"Well, that would be nice."

The next morning our legal department was advised to call Winn early at his hotel, repeat the money offer and ask if he would alter the schedule to permit more verses.

A five-year contract was signed that day.

Eddie Arcaro rode 250 losers before he gained his first victory at the track. Sounds like a slow start.

The 'Ol Redhead

Red Barber was a unique original in the world of broadcasting, especially the broadcasting of sports.

Announcers had become sports reporters – people like Graham McNamee, Bill Stern, Ted Husing, Arch McDonald, Ford Frick and Bill Munday – but Barber did not copy the style or manner of those who preceded him or were his contemporaries.

Barber developed his own "down to earth" style and while many have copied it, and some quite well, none matched his ability to so clearly use words with the Michelangelo skill he possessed in painting a vibrant oral picture.

It was in the Press Room of the St. Louis Cardinals that I first met Red at the 1944 World Series. That was the forgettable Series between the two St. Louis clubs, the Cards and the Browns. He invited me to be interviewed on his pregame Mutual network broadcast.

The invitation came because I was a subject of interest, having flown 16,500 miles from New Delhi, India, on what *Time Magazine* called the "longest sports assignment in history."

At the time, Sgt. Derr was sports editor of the *China-Burma-India Roundup*, the CBI theater newspaper and a weekly reporter of American sports news on the BBC's Far Eastern outlet of

All-India Radio on some 14 wavelengths. General Stilwell had initiated my return to report the series as a morale boost to the troops out there who felt out of touch with our homeland.

The fact that the General had sent me home to give a firsthand report to CBI troops had caught the attention of the media in this country and Barber wanted me to tell his vast radio audience about sports on our side of the world.

Almost two years later Barber replaced Husing as the CBS sports voice. At the time he was the lead broadcaster on games of the Brooklyn Dodgers, which job was to continue in addition to his CBS assignment. He announced he would do baseball and football for the network but would seek experts to describe horse racing, tennis and golf for CBS.

Joe H. Palmer, racing editor of the *N.Y. Herald-Tribune*, was hired to cover the horses, Sarah Palfrey Cooke for tennis and I, with some experience, applied for the golf broadcasts.

"We aren't going to broadcast much golf," Barber told me. "NBC, ABC and Mutual have most of the tournaments. We will bid for some but golf doesn't sell to sponsors so we'll have to wait and see if any golf assignments come on the schedule."

Disappointed, I listened as Red continued.

"However, I plan to start a sports magazine of the air for each evening. I might be able to hire you to write features and the day's highlights to go along with my interviews.

"With your writing experience you could fill that spot for me but I will have to get an okay from my boss, Ed Murrow. Let's go see him."

Murrow, fresh from his triumphant wartime broadcasts from London, had returned to CBS as Vice-President of News, Sports and Special Events, an administrative role he soon relinquished to return to the air.

Barber escorted me around to Murrow's executive office and told Ed what he had in mind. I had two chits in hand. Murrow had been born in North Carolina, as had I and he loved golf with a passion. He was a pretty fair left-handed golfer. When Murrow learned I had covered every Masters since 1935 and was friendly with Jones, Hagen, Snead and Hogan, he nodded to Barber and gave his approval.

Thus began a working education in broadcasting, at the feet of two masters – Barber and Murrow, the best.

Hired as a writer and researcher for Barber, within a few months I was promoted and given a cut in pay. I was given the title of Assistant Sports Director, considered an executive job and eligible for a year-end executive bonus. As a writer I had been called on to prepare sports pieces for other CBS news programs and was paid an extra $25 per story. As an executive my base salary was increased but executives were not eligible for writing fees and there went my extra income.

Barber was still traveling with the Dodgers on road trips and away from the office two weeks at a time. We talked almost daily by phone if there was CBS business needing attention and when he was away Murrow was always there to counsel me.

Meanwhile Barber was sharing with me, through example, his own philosophy about the nuances of sports reporting. As I had been told on my first newspaper job, more than a decade earlier, Red impressed upon me again that a reporter's job was to report. A fan's place was in the stands – neither the press box nor the broadcast booth.

"Be compassionate, even lenient, but be honest in your reporting" was a Barber tenet.

Over the years I heard him often relate the story of his first World Series assignment (1935) and the charge laid down by Commissioner Kenesaw Mountain Landis. I can almost remember it verbatim.

Landis told the broadcaster "Your job is to report, just that. You are not the umpire. You are not the manager. You are not the fan. You have no opinion. Just report."

He prefaced that with an example. "If you see a ball player with a mouthful of chewing tobacco walk over to my box and spit in my face, report from where he started, report how close he came, and if your eyes are good enough, report the accuracy of his delivery. Then report the action of the Commissioner, if any. Report what you saw, not what you think happened."

Red abided by the Commissioner's rules ever after whether it was football, baseball or some other sport he was reporting.

Another thing that made Barber a better reporter was his attention to the answers guests gave to his questions. Too many broadcasters, then and now, fail to do that. They seem so interested in framing their next clever question or else think they know the reply that they move on to the next question. This results in a disjointed conversation. Red listened to his guests and frequently added that little word or two that made the transition to the next question smooth and meaningful.

During his days at CBS we were both embarrassed for an old friend of ours, working on another network, and the dilemma he created one night because he didn't hear the answer.

He was trackside in the winner's circle to interview the owner of the winning horse. The owner came from a family of horse owners, among them her aging mother who had owned many champions. Being courteous and thoughtful, after congratulating the young lady, the reporter asked... "And how is Miss Annie these days?"

Unmindful of her answer, which he probably expected to be the customary "Oh, she's fine," he closed the interview by saying... "That's great. When you see her give her my best."

The owner had answered, "She passed away

two weeks ago."

Barber's style would have prevented that gaff.

Words fascinated Barber. His mother had taught English at a school in Mississippi and Walter Lanier Barber must have been her star pupil. He read many books. His favorites were history and biographies. On a Dodger road trip sometimes he would read three or four.

Unknown words, and there were a few, he looked up in a well-worn dictionary. More important to him than his dictionary were Red's Bible and Book of Common Prayer. As a lay minister in the Episcopal Church he was often called on to conduct services in New York and elsewhere. His sincere sanctity was so respected by others that locker room talk and profanity were avoided by those who knew him well.

He knew the words. Just didn't like to hear them.

One day he was broadcasting the Illinois-Michigan game and the Illinois sports office arranged for a police car to get us from our hotel to the stadium. It was Band Day at the game and the town of Champaign-Urbana was filled with dozens of school youngsters and their horns and drums.

The cruiser arrived for us and a bulging officer directed us into the car. Red sat up front with the talkative cop. His every other word was profane and every noun was preceded by an active adjective. The assembling bands were denounced as we flew by. Red could see the speedometer, I couldn't. Red told him we had plenty of time, take it easy.

The needle throbbed as it held its pace. More bands, more school kids, more cursing but we landed safely at the stadium.

The three-mile trip took maybe four minutes and as we deplaned the policeman produced an autograph book and asked Red to sign. With no comment he did, but I knew he was upset.

Then Red produced a piece of paper and asked for the autograph of the driver and the name of his supervising officer. You could see the story developing, he'd tell 'em at the station that Red Barber had asked for his autograph. What a switch.

When he handed it back, Red quietly said: "Sir, you are a disgrace as an officer. You could have killed some of those children back there in the bands. I told you I was in no hurry. I am writing your superior and requesting that you be censured."

That was the day Red gave the cop a ticket.

Politically unhappy at developments with the Dodgers, Red accepted a bid to move cross town and broadcast Yankee games. CBS named me to succeed him as head of radio and television sports. In some manner Red became obsessed that I had been disloyal and for several years our relationship was strained.

Knowing I was innocent of his imagined transgressions this bothered me a great deal. Eventually our differences disappeared and that made all the more important to me a note Red penned to congratulate me after some golf tournament. It was saved.

In his later years I tried never to miss his Friday morning commentaries on National Public Radio. With access to more publications, when I noticed an article I knew would interest him, I would send it to him, saying no reply necessary. Nevertheless a short penned note of thanks would follow in a few days.

The transition from behind the mike to behind the desk was easy for Red when he joined CBS. He was a persuasive negotiator on sports events rights, had an easy understanding of sponsors and developed a cadre of good young broadcasters.

He was a busy man but generous with his time in his church work, giving benefit performances as a talented emcee and in counseling fledgling broadcasters, many of whom became famous. Perhaps the best known of these was Vin Scully, who learned at Ebbetts Field and went West with the Dodgers.

There was one administrative rule Barber insisted upon. He wanted all mail answered or acknowledged without delay. Most of our mail fell into one of three or four categories and in time we could recognize these and answer with a form reply. Red composed standard replies to the standard questions.

The secretary could prepare these for Red's or my signature. If it was not routine, unanswerable by a stock reply, she was instructed to acknowledge its receipt and say Mr. Barber was out of the office and would reply when he returned. He considered it discourteous to not acknowledge all correspondence.

This worked well most of the time but there was once when we were both in Miami for 10 days at Orange Bowl time when the system broke down. While we were away a recently hired secretary had received an offer of a job in Hollywood. This was not too surprising because she had a figure that made Bridget Bardot look like a boy.

She called us in Miami and said she would need to leave right away. Red didn't want to chill her career move and was able to convince her to stay on the job until I returned and could hire a replacement.

Everything looked in good order on my return. Our desks were clear and only a few late letters, but mail usually was slack during the holidays. I reluctantly sent her westward.

In late January both Red and I ran into people who asked why they had received no response to their letters. We were baffled and others continued to ask about our replies.

Red asked me to call the ex-secretary and see if she knew why "What about the letters these people sent?" I asked.

"Oh, they're all there. They are in the file cabinet. If I couldn't answer them I filed them, like you said. You'll find them in the second drawer under "U" for unanswered."

There must have been 20 of them. Now Red got a little perturbed about that. He didn't swear, but he seemed to approve when I did. Every time, thereafter, when I saw a dizzy blonde in a TV show I swore again...filed under "U," my word.

Barber had a great sense of humor, at times, and he was a master of the practical joke. One time we had broadcast the heated rivalry game of Florida and Georgia Tech at Atlanta and Tech was nationally ranked and hoping for a bowl bid. The Gators took a surprising 7-0 lead in the first quarter, but when Tech unleashed its air attack the final score was something like 35-7.

As was his custom, as time permitted, Red would stop by after a game and express his appreciation to the coach. We walked into Coach Bobby Dodd's office and with an embarrassed, apologetic look on his face, opened the conversation by saying, "Bobby, I'm sorry but there was nothing we could do about it. The lines went out at the end of the first quarter and I guess all the bowl people think you lost, 7-0."

Dodd was devastated. He had counted on the national broadcast assuring him of the Bowl bid. Red enjoyed his torment for a couple of minutes and then confessed his joke. Bobby was still in shock when we left the stadium. Red enjoyed it.

Barber had his thinning hair trimmed at a barbershop in Radio City, regularly and by appointment. I had never had a barber where you had to have an appointment. With me it was go in and wait until a chair opened up.

One day when he said he was going to see his barber, and I was in need of a haircut, he suggested I go with him. When we arrived there was a chair open, Red introduced me to this barber and went over several chairs to his appointment.

After the cloth was draped around my shoulders, this man ran his hand through my hair and casually remarked, as barbers do, "Yes, I think that would look pretty good on you." What did he mean, I asked. "The crew cut," he said.

"But I don't want a crew cut. Just a regular trim."

"Yes, I know, but I'm sure you'll like it."

Rising from the chair in this fancy shop. I said, "Let's get this straight. I don't want a crew cut."

Across the way I could see Barber and his man laughing. Red had whispered to my barber that I was too bashful to suggest it, maybe too old for that style, but that I really wanted a crew cut. Regardless of my reluctance he should go ahead, whack it off to a crew cut length. My last trip to Red's barbershop.

When we went out of town for a broadcast

one of my duties was to see that the egg-timers were packed.

Always with the listener in mind, and knowing that not all listeners stay in earshot of the radio throughout a broadcast, Red devised a way to accommodate them.

In front of us in the booth we placed a three-minute egg-timer – the kind that had glass bulbs, top and bottom, filled with fine granular sand. Red would give the score and again flip the timer. Repeat as needed.... every three minutes.

One final recollection about the Ol' Redhead. He used some home-grown Southern expressions to describe baseball in Brooklyn, but the Dodger fans worshiped the red-headed Rebel. He could talk about a controversy developing into rhubarb and they knew he wasn't talking about a vegetable.

He could describe a pitcher who was sailing along in his comfort zone as being in "the catbird seat" and they knew he was in control.

But unlike later broadcasters, Barber didn't ponder over these colorful descriptions the night before. They all came to him naturally, inspired by the events of the moment. Today some broadcasters spend hours thinking up clever sayings and then looking for a place to slip them in as "ad libs."

Barber's were just Barber, undeniably the best of his day and maybe the best there'll ever be.

His hands may have been the largest I ever saw on any man. When Laurie Auchterlonie extended a hand to greet you, you extended yours wondering what shape it would be in when you disengaged. It was always a surprise when his hand turned out to be firm, but with the softness of a violin player.

Maybe that was not so surprising for like the world-class musician. Auchterlonie was a world-class craftsman whose massive hands were used to shape custom made golf clubs for 70 years. An Auchterlonie club was a prized possession and his woodenheaded putter enjoyed decades of popularity. He was two years behind in orders when he died in the early 90's.

I first met the talented Scot at his golf shop, across the road from the famed St. Andrews course. This was 1948 when I was visiting the cradle of golf with Robert Neill, a scratch player who had been the Scottish Closed Champion just before the Second World War and who lived in Glasgow.

Neill had been stationed in New Delhi during a part of my service in India and our friendship continued afterwards.

Before our first round at St. Andrews, Bob had used his influence to obtain entrance for me into the private catacombs of the famous home of the Royal and Ancient. It was a moving experience to look at the historic relics from earlier golfers.

"When we finish today I want to take you across the street to Auchterlonie's golf shop and you can meet the man who knows more about club-making than any man in Scotland. That's young Laurie Auchterlonie.

"You met his father, Willie, earlier today. Willie is the Honorary Professional at St. Andrews. Willie's father was that before him and since the appointment is for life, Willie will have that title until he dies. And then, I expect, they will elect Laurie as the Honorary Professional," Bob explained.

Willie won the British Open (there was no other) in 1893 and lived into his 90's. As Neill predicted, at the age of 60, upon the death of his father, Laurie did receive that honor. He was Honorary Professional for life.

Golf was his whole life but it was early golf equipment that was his passion, a passion inherited from his father and grandfather. He became recognized as the authentic word on early golf clubs, balls and equipment.

One night Laurie and his wife, Bea, were visiting in my home at Pinehurst. Laurie had become quite crippled by this time, five hip operations and replacements having failed to restore his mobility. When I stopped at the hotel to pick him up I learned how difficult it was for him to enter an automobile. He backed into the front seat and then asked me to lift his legs and feet and swing them around in front of him.

His feet were large, too, for he was a big man. His feet did not impress me as much as his huge, rugged hands; for I knew I would not be shaking feet with him, only hands.

Naturally the conversation centered on golf. Some time earlier I had purchased a handful of wooden-shafted clubs at an auction in Maine. They were not bought to go into a collection. I wanted the wooden shafts. Anyway, they were left-handed irons.

After picking out the straightest of the lot I sawed off the mashie club head. I trimmed down the shaft, shaving both sides until it had a wee bit of flexibility. Then I inserted the shaft into a solid brass putter head, whose size and shape intrigued me.

The putter looked good, just enough give in the shaved down shaft to let me feel the club moving through. It didn't do a lot for my putting but it looked good and felt good. I was quite pleased with my effort and thought I'd show my own craftsmanship to the world's most celebrated club-maker.

Still seated, Laurie took it and swished it through the air, slowly and then with more zoom. I waited for his judgment.

"Well, you've done quite remarkable in having it balanced. It's heavy and you've set the shaft in quite true. I think you may have shaved the shaft a bit too much as it has quite a whip to it."

Not bad, I thought. Not real good, but not bad.

"Where is the club head you sawed off?"

It's now a paper weight I told him as I went to my den to retrieve it. The head had not been important, it was the shaft I needed.

When I handed the iron club head to Laurie, he turned it over and moved it to brighter light. He looked long at the maker's logo; the identification stamped on the back, and sat silent for a couple of moments.

Then, wearing a look of sadness and horror, he said: "Lad, you've ruined a very valuable club. This is the stamp of (a name with which I was not familiar). That club was made nearly 100 years ago and would have been very Collectable."

He was hurt, and so was I when I learned its value.

Seeking expert approval of my reconstructed putter, instead I had encountered a withering look of regret.

Before his crippled hips ended his playing days, Laurie was a delightful companion on the course. He could add stories of early golf that one doesn't find in books. Some were personal recollections and others had been handed down to him by his father and grandfather who had apprenticed under old Tom Morris.

On one such day the matter of conceding putts came up. Laurie was not only a traditionalist in a sport where tradition is extremely high, but, being from the home of the R & A, he was a stickler for the rules.

Remember this the next time your worthy opponent looks at you entreatingly when his ball rests 23 inches from the cup.

Quoting an early Scot, Laurie said the thing to say is:

"IF 'TIS CLOSE ENOUGH TO GIVE,

'TIS CLOSE ENOUGH TO PUTT. PLAY."

Big hands, big heart, big man. I loved him.

Knowing more education would be beneficial and knowing there was no money for college tuition, I looked for another barter opportunity. If the newspaper was willing to swap my work for a trade, maybe I should step up my goals and seek higher learning.

Near my home was an outstanding Catholic school, Belmont Abbey College. It enjoyed an excellent academic rating and also had a good football team. The coach was Howard "Humpy" Wheeler, former stalwart at the University of Illinois. Wheeler knew the advantages of getting favorable publicity for any team, but more especially for a winning one. Recruiting was much easier if prospective players knew your record and your schedule.

Traditionally the Abbey fielded good teams but they received scant publicity. It was not yet the practice for small schools to have a Sports Information Director on staff to send out pre-game and post-game stories to the press.

In my work for *The Gazette* I often covered Abbey practices and games, usually with their football team, for that was the sport where they excelled. They sometimes had good basketball teams and Al McGuire was once the cage coach at Abbey.

During my visits I came to know Coach Wheeler quite well. He had been a national star and we didn't have too many of those around Gaston County. One day I broached the subject of adding to my work schedule the duties of an S.I.D., if I could swap my work as their Sports Information Director for more education as a non-enrolled Abbey student.

Coach Wheeler liked the idea...and the price was right, as far as getting a person to help publicize his football teams. He took up the matter with Father Cuthbert E. Allen, his president, and he liked the idea too.

Next they called in Father Gregory Eichenlaub, who headed the English department and who had been on the faculty of several large Catholic schools

Father Gregory agreed to coach me in all phases of English, from composition to comprehension. For the next three years, in addition to my day job (I was now being paid $12 a week) at *The Gazette*, I visited the Abbey three nights a week for my tutored English. All the while I was flooding the area media outlets with stories about Coach Wheeler's Red Crusaders.

I was lucky again.

Never did I have to sit in class. Never did I have to compete with my peers and never did I have to worry about term papers or graduating.

Actually, the first college classroom I was ever in came in the early days of WWII when the regular instructor drew a low draft number, No. 48, and left for military duty. They asked me to teach his class until a qualified instructor could be located. So I took over. I was finally in a college journalism classroom...and I was the teacher.

Lucky again, I guess.

He was a successful Wall Street investment broker, wore dark conservative three-piece suits, shielded his feelings behind round beige-trimmed glasses...but Clifford Roberts was really a warm, kind, and decent man behind that saturnine façade.

Roberts was once described by a noted English journalist as looking like "a delegate to an undertaker's convention."

No one could deny that it was the popularity of Bob Jones and his charismatic career that "made" the Masters, but in Cliff Roberts he had the other half of the equation that assured its success.

Through his stewardship of the Masters, where he and Jones shared the responsibility of making it successful, Roberts was a powerful influence over golf for half a century.

There were those – and some were players – who spoke unkindly of the man, damning his defense of his own turf, but even his detractors respected his goal of perfection. Chipped dishes he discarded, unless he found a way to make them better.

As a reporter long before television, I respected him, but did not fear him. I don't know why he chose to accept me behind his public screen, but he did and it was appreciated.

Some time in the early fifties he was walking in mid-morning toward his apartment at the far north end of the clubhouse. We exchanged hellos and to my surprise he asked if I would join him for a cup of tea.

As I departed he said that he usually had tea and crumpets there about this time each morning and asked me to drop in the next day if I cared to. I did.

Thus began a nearly daily ritual that extended some 20 years. We were sitting in his quarters during the first round of the 1956 tournament. Through his windows we could see the large scoreboard between the 10th and 18th fairways.

Roberts called to my attention that the very talented young amateur from San Francisco, Ken Venturi, had been put on the board after starting birdie, birdie, "I'm glad he could play this year." he remarked.

A few minutes later we noticed another birdie for him at the third, which we duly appreciated. But when Venturi scored a birdie deuce at the tough fourth, Roberts turned to me and said "Well, Bob said we should televise all 18 holes. It looks like he was right."

That was the first year of television and only the last three and a half holes were covered, just a portion of what Jones had said should be done.

Another year, 1970, my back and legs were causing me a great deal of pain. This was a week before I underwent a lower spine operation – a double laminectomy and a foramenotomy at the fourth and fifth lumbar vertebrae. So I was hurting.

After tea I asked Roberts if I might be permitted to use a golf cart to travel to and from my tower at the 15th hole. Those hills were steep even then, worse now.

"Well, I'll have to think about that. We didn't want carts running all over the course." He said I should check later with his secretary, Helen Harris. That was not a yes, only a hope.

Later, I checked with Mrs. Harris and she handed me a note, on Masters memo paper, which I still have. It reads:

"To Whom it may concern. John Derr has permission to use this cart en route to and from the 15th green."

CR

"P.S. John, please don't drive on the greens."

Once, after we had played the big course, we moved over to the par three to conclude our day's play. If he had played decently on the big course, Roberts often suggested the short course for dessert.

That day, with uncommon good luck, I was able to shoot three pars, three bogeys and three birdies for an even par 27.

"This may be the last time I'll suggest you

come over here," Cliff said as we trudged in. And it was.

During January in those days I organized and ran the Jamaica Jamboree pro-am tournaments in Montego Bay, using the Tryall and Half-Moon courses.

One morning at Tryall, Dugan Aycock came to the first tee where I was watching the foursomes tee off and said "There's a friend of yours in the pro shop asking about you."

There stood Mr. Roberts. Dressed not in his three-piece Wall Street suit, but wearing a semi-loud Caribbean shirt and sports slacks. He had caught a winter cold and couldn't shake it, so he came to Montego Bay to let the sun bake it out.

That afternoon, with some of the Stateside writers who were on the junket, we played Tryall. Jimmy Demaret had given Roberts an aerosol can of some magic fluid that if sprayed on the ball at each tee was supposed to eliminate hooks and slices. He enjoyed trying it out, knowing it was not legal, and I might add it was not very effective, either.

Three days later we had the "pro only" division of our nine-day safari. Herb Graffis, Smith Barrier and Oscar Fraley and another couple of writers loaded up in carts and rode out to watch the pros.

There was one hole that had a fairly deep, wide drainage ditch down the entire left side, crossing short of the green. The fairway tilted to the left. The scorecard identified this ditch as a hazard, a water hazard during the rainy season. This day it was dry and the floor had scads of little stones that washed down from the hills during December rains.

We observed a pro go down into the ditch, toss aside a few stones and play to the green and take two putts. We moved on about the course but when I checked the scoreboard I saw he had posted a four, not the four plus two penalty strokes. And he had signed an incorrect score and disqualified himself.

Jack Round, from Toronto, was my scoreboard official and I asked him to round up the 40 other pros, who were eating in the grill and see how many had made the same mistake.

Meanwhile I walked down to the seaside casino to meet Mr. Roberts for lunch. I explained that a scoreboard incident had delayed me, and told him about the disqualification and that Jack Round was checking the others. I thought there might be others, not realizing it was a hazard or maybe seeing someone in the group ahead commit the same breach.

We had not quite finished our sandwiches when Round showed up. He wore a troubled look.

Apologetically he approached our table and said: "We have a real bad situation. All of the pros are in and I've asked each of them if they moved stones in that ditch."

He hesitated, almost as though afraid to

continue.

"Yes," I said, "and how many did you find?"

He looked straight at me and said "There were 19. What shall I do?"

With the gesture given by a baseball umpire, I raised my hand and swung it up and out.

"They are out. All 19 disqualified."

Mr. Roberts took another swallow from his glass of iced tea, looked at me and said: "My lord. You just threw out half of your field...and at Augusta they call me a dictator."

Roberts had a sense of humor, just didn't use it much.

NOTE: (This I just remembered and it might fit somewhere)...

Cadillac and Travelers arranged to produce a 60-minute film of the 1958 Masters. Horton Smith and I were to edit miles of footage to fit the time. I was to narrate.

When we showed the green print to Roberts at NBC studios in New York, there was one player none of us could identify. We didn't need his name for the film but Roberts asked who he was and neither Smith nor I could be sure.

"I know he's from South America," I said.

Roberts said that was not true but offered no name.

"You should know, Cliff," I told him "After all, you invited him and you should know who he is."

"I don't recall who he is but I'll bet you two dollars he is not from South America," was Roberts' retort.

"You're on."

That afternoon, after Roberts had left the studio, we brought Fred Corcoran in to identify him. Fred knew instantly he was an English amateur.

A week later I got a letter acknowledging receipt of my check and error. His letter said... "The cards have not been going well in my games with the Chief (which name he always used for President Eisenhower) so your two dollars is now in the White House kitchen fund. Thanks, C.R."

There's an old axiom that says in life you have to play the hand that's dealt you. Just play to win. In golf tournaments it's the same. You have to play in the grouping to which you are assigned and hope for the best. One can't choose who will be your fellow competitors.

In the early 1950's I was invited to play in the Press Division of the National Baseball Players Championship in Miami. This was a great event, run by a former sports writer, Bill Wallace, and sponsored by the Greater Miami Chamber of Commerce.

Stars, former stars and wannabees always showed up for this fun weekend. It was scheduled the week before spring training camps opened so everyone was anxious for one final blowout.

Interested in learning with whom I was to play I dashed out to the Miami Springs course to look at the pairings board. I wasn't disappointed.

Al Lopez from Tampa, manager of the Chicago White Sox and one of the better players, would be joined by Tommy Byrne from North Carolina who southpawed for the Yankees. The other player was a young bandy-legged fireplug-sized catcher from St. Louis, who toiled behind the plate for the Yankees – Yogi Berra.

The grouping suited me fine. I had a major league manager, a winning pitcher and a colorful catcher. All we needed was a hitter, but instead they had me.

Things went well on the front nine. Lopez, the best player of the group and a threat for the overall championship, scored a stroke or two over par. I was out in a surprising 38.

"You could be the medalist in your division," Lopez said, when he picked up an orange juice at the turn. "If you can get one or two birdies, that should do it."

Berra heard the challenge and became vocally supportive.

Pars on the first three inward holes preceded a drive behind a palm tree and a bogey. Three putts cost another one.

On the long par five 15th, still feeling down after those two bogeys, my drive was not too good. The second shot put me within a seven iron of the elevated green. I took the club, carefully adjusted my grip and stance, and settled in to play the shot.

At that precise moment I felt a slap on my left shoulder like it might have been someone trying to kill a June bug. I flinched and stepped back.

It was the exuberant Berra, showing support such as a baseball player might to a batter going out to face a swift pitcher and you'd encourage him "hit it out of here." I think his words were "hit it close" but I was too shocked to be sure.

The seven iron sailed over the green, down a steep slope and this was another bogey. Meanwhile Lopez was explaining that in golf you sometimes show your support by being quiet.

On the short 16th I sank a 20-foot birdie putt and regrouped my nerves.

On the strength of the birdie I was first up on the 17th. This was a shortish par four. Its difficulty lay not in its length, but there was a stream, a creek, or a canal or something that diagonally bisected the fairway. It might be possible to clear it on the right side but there was ample landing space on the left as it was farther to the stream that way.

I moved to the left side of the tee to aim right and draw the ball back with my pesky hook, getting closer to the green.

By now about 200 fans had become our walking gallery. Some of them were Tampa friends of Lopez, but most had come to see Yogi. Byrne had a few followers and Peggy had joined us at the previous hole as my gallery of one. Soon she wished she hadn't.

Again I teed my ball, took my stance and prepared to swing.

Buoyed by my birdie the ebullient Berra was back in voice.

"Wait, John," he yelled, before I had moved the club.

"Do you know that down the left side it's out of bounds?"

Peggy turned her head. She couldn't watch. My ball went left but not enough to reach the OB stakes. Instead it was in amongst some scrubby pines and low hanging bushes.

We found it but with a restricted swing all I wanted to do was get back to the fairway. It came out too well, bounded up the edge of the stream and disappeared.

This time we didn't find the ball. It had barely been moving and we thought if it stopped on the footpath bordering the creek it might be playable. Four players, four caddies and about 20 volunteers could not find it, so Lopez said, "It's in the water for sure. Add one and take your drop." I did.

The others had already played to the green before I had and when we reached it, three balls were on and Berra was a few feet off. The caddie pulled out Berra's left-handed wedge. Berra played from both sides. The wedge and putter from the left side, the others right. But there was no Berra in sight.

Lopez asked the caddie, "Where's Yogi?"

The caddie shrugged his aching shoulders as if to say he didn't know and didn't care. Someone in the gallery said... "He's back down there in the creek, looking for your ball."

When it was explained to him the ball had

been abandoned and could not be played, even if found, Yogi rejoined us and reluctantly completed the hole.

My 78 left me second low qualifier among the press and next day we began match play. Match play was new to Berra.

In his first match Yogi was beaten, 3 and 2. He dropped into the "beaten eight" and faced another foe in the afternoon. Again Yogi lost, 3 and 2.

Afterwards I saw Yogi studying the pairings board. He did not see his name listed for Saturday play and he tried to find out why.

Chairman Wallace stood nearby. Yogi asked him, "Who do I play tomorrow?"

"How did you do this afternoon, Yogi?"

"I got beat."

"Well, you are finished if you lost two matches."

Yogi looked perplexed. "I don't understand why," he said.

"If we go into Chicago and lose the first two games we still play the next two."

He was a scrapper, that Yogi. I loved his attitude.

In case you are interested, I won the Press Division but not before two surprises. After winning both Friday matches I was slated to play a Philadelphia writer on Saturday. He came up to me in the grill, explained that he also was the racing writer and had to cover the stakes race at Hialeah Saturday.

"I'm playing real well right now and probably would win tomorrow if we played, but since I have to get out to the track early, would you be interested in forfeiting to me?"

"No," hiding my shock at his nerve. "You may win but I didn't come here to forfeit."

Before I left the club I ran into Jackie Robinson. I was doing TV direction on the Dodgers and knew all the Brooklyn players well. I told him what the Philadelphia writer proposed.

Jackie asked what was my tee time. I told him and since he had won twice he would be playing Saturday also. "I won't be able to be there myself but you'll have rooting support."

The next morning when we arrived at the first tee, Monte Irvin, Roy Campanella (a favorite of mine) and every Brooklyn Dodger who had been eliminated had on his walking shoes. There were about seven or eight of them, some black, some white, all shouting encouragement to me. It got quite funny. No matter the length of my putt the ball would barely be rolling when the chorus of "get in, get in" came forth.

It was not too good a match. I won, 5 and 4, and he got to Hialeah in time for the daily double. Good riddance.

Of course this meant I would be in the finals Sunday. I was to play my good friend, Jimmy Burns, sports editor of *The Miami Herald*. Jimmy was a few years older than I and he suggested he would prefer to forfeit, to not play.

"Come on, Jimmy, let's play. It's been too long since we've played and I would enjoy being with you."

Sunday he showed up but suggested we go one or two holes and he'd forfeit due to exhaustion. He had played five straight days and surely was tired. I didn't want to win on a forfeit so we began.

I won the first three holes and it looked like we might not go too far, but I was enjoying my visit with my old friend.

We walked and talked and kept on playing, just the two of us and our caddies. No Dodger fan club this day.

On the 15th hole the young caddie who had been with me all week, called me aside and offered some advice and shocking information.

"Mister, you'd better quit talking and start playing. Do you know you are one down?"

I had no idea, but thought I was several up.

Even though he was a dear friend I didn't want to lose.

Jimmy was getting tired and I paid more attention to my business and won, 2 and 1. And a good tip for the alert caddie.

Cricket, somewhere around the house, maybe in the attic, there is a cardboard box with a big engraved silver tray and eight silver tumblers, unused. I say silver, but before you try to sell as silver, put some vinegar on the back and test.

They are the spoils from

  one forfeit I wouldn't make

  and one I wouldn't accept.

My heart is heavy today for I have just lost the dearest friend and pal I ever had. My father spent many hours with me, tramping through the fields following our bird dogs and standing on river banks waiting for the fish to bite. He was a sportsman in the fullest meaning of the word – a sportsman who believed in the conservation of game.

It was while roaming the fields with him, not carrying a gun – for I never mastered the art of shooting, that I used to hunt Indian arrowheads. We'd walk along and talk of Indians and of the people who had hunted those same fields years before us.

While fishing we'd often hear birds whistling and watch them flying overhead. Then he'd tell me about these creatures that seemed to be enjoying life as much as we were. He didn't rely on books to let me learn about nature. He took that job himself with much interest.

About four years ago he hunted his last time. After that he spent many hours with his dogs and also was busy with raising pheasants and quail to turn loose on his 85-acre farm. He never lost his love for the outdoor life and just a few weeks ago we were planning a short fishing trip this summer.

There will be no more tramps through the fields together for us, nor will we get the thrill of seeing each other land a fish; but there will always be memories for me of the happy days we spent together, learning first-hand what it meant to be a sportsman.

Those are happy memories and cherished ones. But today, I am sad.

This was my daily column, written for The Greensboro Daily News *of March 29, 1941. Thirty minutes earlier I had received a phone call telling me he had died. I wrote this memory column and left on my sad trip to his home.*

Charlie Nicklaus was sitting behind a thick support pillar, deep in the mezzanine balcony of a mid-Manhattan hotel the first time I ever saw him. And he was not very happy. One might even say his German dander was up.

It was the night of the annual awards dinner of the Metropolitan Golf Writers Association, an event of national significance as all golfing champions came in person to accept their awards.

We were at that time of the evening when those most interested in the program, especially the families, arrive early to check out their seat location.

The reception for dais guests was still going on in a salon near the ballroom as the host writers mingled with their celebrated champion guests. Boutonnieres had been inserted in the lapels of both. I regretted leaving the pulsating excitement but I needed to check on some friends who had been assigned balcony seats.

As I walked into the half-filled upper room I noticed this gentleman and a party of several couples, decidedly upset. I moved to him and asked if something was wrong.

"These aren't very good seats," he replied. "We are relatives of Jack Nicklaus and we came from Columbus, Ohio, to see the awards. From these seats we can barely see a corner of the dais."

Apparently he correctly deduced from my floral bouquet that I was an association member and could do something about their horrible seating. The dinner was a sell-out, as it usually was, and I had no way of moving that post or moving their table.

At that moment I spotted the service captain in charge of that area. I called him over and explained that this man's son was the National Amateur champion and these folks had come from Columbus to see him honored...and now they could not see.

"Just a minute" was his response. How often one hears that from a waitperson and usually it is followed by "I'm sorry I can do nothing."

This captain was different. He saw a way to juggle the tables, move a couple this way and a couple that, and he got "line of sight relief" for the entire Nicklaus family, including Uncle Frank, an Ohio judge. It was not good, but better.

By this time I had met them all and went on to seek my friends, whose view was also obstructed, but that happens with a full house sometimes.

Mr. Nicklaus was most grateful and a long friendship began that night in the balcony.

Charlie Nicklaus was a wonderful fellow. How wonderful you may judge by this story which was told to me by an Ohio sports writer – not by

Jack and certainly not by Charlie.

Young Nicklaus won the Ohio Open when he was very young. This made him the odds-on favorite in every schoolboy and amateur event he entered. Jack entered the Ohio Amateur in Cleveland and, as expected, sailed through his early matches. In the semi-finals he faced another Columbus lad, a young man from a broken home and of limited resources.

After a stirring match, he beat Jack, one up.

As they walked off the green, Charlie strode over and congratulated the victor and wished him well the next day in the finals.

Knowing the lad's circumstances Charlie asked if any of his family would be coming from Columbus to cheer him on in the finals.

"No," he replied. "My mother will be working and my sister has no way to come here."

Charlie asked him to call his mother and ask her to get off work and come see her son play for the title. "It just happens I have two round-trip air tickets for tomorrow and I will not be using them. You call her and I'll see that the tickets get into her hands tonight when I get home."

This best epitomizes the kind of fellow Charlie Nicklaus was. Few of us would be so gracious. I loved him. Jack came from fine stock, as you can see.

Charlie did miscalculate badly one time, though.

Early during a Doral tournament he approached me by the putting green and said he had a favor to ask.

"You know I think Jack might listen better to you than anyone I can name. He's been taking flying lessons and has it in his head that he wants to buy his own plane. I wish you'd find a way to talk with him this week and tell him you think that's a foolish idea."

Surprised at this hitherto unknown influence I had on his son, I told Charlie I didn't see how I could. "First off," I said, "Jack could tell me it was none of my business and he would be correct."

If an opportunity arose, I told Charlie I would try to get him talking about flying and the plane and maybe I could sneak in my demurrer.

Friday night I stopped in the Eastern Air Lines hospitality suite and soon Jack arrived. Eastern was a television sponsor and Jack appeared as their spokesman, so it was a good gamble he'd show up at their party. In time Jack made it around to my side of the room and I had the chance to ask the question I had come there to ask.

"What's this about you getting your own plane, like Arnie has?"

"Been looking into it," Jack said. "I have to

fly a lot to exhibitions and meetings and I could do a lot more if I flew myself." He had made his point but he opened the door. I gave him all the reasons I thought might discourage him from making his purchase.

With that all-knowing, confident, sometimes cocky smile he often flourished in those days, Nicklaus looked over his shoulder to me as he walked away and said, "We'll just have to see."

Saturday when I first saw Charlie I was able to report on the conversation.

"I don't think you need to worry, Charlie. He's still thinking about it but he didn't seem adamant...said he'd have to see. So maybe the talk helped," I assured him.

Charlie seemed pleased and said, "Thanks. I thought he might listen to you."

He did. He also listened to the plane salesman and on the front sports page of the Sunday *Miami Herald* the headline on a small story said:

"NICKLAUS BUYS JET PLANE."

So much for influence.

"Can We Rehearse It?"

During the 1971 Ryder Cup matches at the old Warson Country Club in St. Louis, an early fall cool spell descended on the area about mid-day of the first day's play. By the time our television staff was scheduled to check out the facilities on the announce towers, the temperature had dropped almost 20 degrees.

Since the event was being played in mid-September, our usual source of schoolboy golf teams to serve as spotters and scorers was not available.

At ordinary tournaments, where our communication lines were more extensive or sometimes, as at Augusta, more or less permanent, one might not necessarily need an observer on the tower. But because of the format of the Ryder Cup it was almost obligatory to have extra eyes to double-check the number of strokes taken on the hole. No guesses allowed.

Our producer, aware of the shortage of non-tower help, reported at the morning production meeting he would find personnel some place by rehearsal time and to proceed as normal.

And he did. When I arrived at my location behind the 17th green, waiting for me there was a young member of the LPGA Tour, and I do believe their cutest and almost their youngest.

"They asked me to come out here to help you

with the scoring and player identification," she said. "You'll have to tell me what you want me to do"

Great, I thought, this is quite an improvement.

Then I looked down at my hands. In addition to my briefcase and binoculars I had supplied myself with one of those hard, waxed carton buckets from Kentucky Fried Chicken, the 13-piece size.

Did I have a problem? Not yet.

The affable young lady professional, looking even more demure and innocent, and I ascended the tower, me somewhat clumsily with both hands full. We opened up the folding chairs and placed them at the makeshift table/desk on which rested the microphone.

This was the time, I figured. It had to be now.

"I need to explain something to you," I told her as I put the KFC bucket alongside the left side of my chair. She was seated to my right.

"As you can tell the weather is getting cold. We'll be up here about three hours. I'm not blessed with the most cooperative kidneys in cold weather.

"Since I can't leave the tower I've brought this bucket up here, to use in case of an emergency. I may not need it. But, just so you won't think I am some sort of an exhibitionist nut, if I feel the need to use this bucket, I'll signal you to watch down the fairway. I'll use the bucket and we'll go on with the broadcast.

"I apologize for being so frank about this but I didn't want to shock you if I have to use it. Is that okay?"

With her bright eyes confirming her vocal assent she said "Sure. No problem. Are you going to rehearse it?"

End of story...almost.

"FOUL BALLS COST YOU"

Sports instructors frequently try to find a motion or an action with which the pupil is already familiar as the best way to get the pupil to understand the desired motion.

Ben Hogan in his great instruction book, *The Modern Fundamentals of Golf,* writes that "the correct motion of the right arm and hand in the impact area resembles the motion an infielder makes when he throws half sidearm, half underhand to first after fielding a ground ball."

With an illustration later in his book, Hogan explains the correct integrated motion the two arms and hands make as they approach the ball as resembling the old two-handed basketball pass.

Other golf instructors have used other examples to put a familiar picture or action in the pupil's mind. Percy Boomer, a resourceful British professional, who wrote an excellent book and was an accomplished teacher, tried to get his pupils to relate their swings to the rhythm of dancers, gracefully going from one position to another. Grace and rhythm, two requisites of ballroom dancing, were equally a necessity for good golf, according to Boomer.

And we are all familiar with the oft-quoted suggestion from Sam Snead that one's grip should be no tighter than one would be holding a little bird in your hand, don't squeeze.

Recently I heard a new "thought suggestion" that could be added to ways to get across a point.

A former major league baseball player brought with him his young son, also a good baseballer, when he came to play with me. The lad had only recently taken up this sport but was anxious to learn, so he could join his dad.

After a visit to the range we approached the first tee.

Understandably he took a batter's position when he faced the ball, lowered his club and took a mighty swing. Off to the right the first ball skittered as the breeze from the swing zipped through the air.

This will be a long nine holes, I thought.

"Not so hard," his dad said. "Just swing. Don't kill it."

A second effort was only marginally better and I was glad when the game was postponed in favor of more work at the range.

I went with them, feeling sorry for both.

It was there I heard one of the best instructions for a beginner I had ever heard. And it worked.

"Son," the dad explained, "in golf you try for singles...not home runs. In this sport one foul means you are out."

Like magic, the lad slowed down his swing.

He could relate to trying only for singles to keep the ball in play.

Impressed by his improvement, and with the first tee empty, I suggested we put his lesson to the test by playing a few holes. This was the boy's first time at a legitimate course and when he parred the fourth hole, I knew the lesson had taken.

What a revelation. A single over second base is so much better than a home run foul ball. Try it sometime.

In the television trade, veteran producer Frank Chirkinian is known as the "Benevolent Dictator" for his award-winning coverage of golf for CBS. No man ever deserved his nickname better or relished it as much as the Armenian alien.

Millions of fans owe a round of applause for the innovative artistry with which he captured the excitement and nuances of tournament golf over many decades.

I lost the first argument with him. I also lost the last one and every one in between. It's probably incorrect to call our differences "arguments." You didn't argue with Frank. Let's call them DOO – differences of opinion. Losing one of these early one April morning in a Greensboro hotel room saved my life. So, I owe him some applause, too.

Our first DOO occurred in the final round of the 1958 PGA championship at the Llanerch CC, outside of Philadelphia. Frank lived and worked in Ben Franklin's hometown and was surrounded by colleagues from WCAU, who thought it was wonderful that a local boy had been given this responsibility on the network.

From my home in Maine I had driven down to be one of the announcers. This created something of an awkward situation, for many of the technical crew had worked with and for me over the past few years, but now I was no longer in charge.

A few months before, an event known in broadcast parlance as a "reorganization," had resulted in my being replaced as head of CBS Sports administration.

This was after I had successfully negotiated to bring CBS the broadcast rights to the Masters, the Kentucky Derby, the Indianapolis 500, and after a summer of almost daily contact with Commissioner Bert Bell at his Atlantic City summer home, I obtained the rights to all NFL games, except two teams.

New administrative personnel had moved into the power slots at CBS and naturally new faces were brought in. My power base had weakened. Red Barber had gone to the Yankees and even Ed Murrow was feeling the first wave of rejection from the top.

Their right to make changes could not be challenged but I did succeed in getting the earlier accusation of "insubordination" removed from my personnel file. It was untrue and unfair. That was eliminated and a longer severance negotiated.

Judge for yourself if "insubordination" was a just cause. A year earlier, after Jack Fleck beat Ben Hogan in the playoff for the 1957 Open, Fleck was invited to Washington to play a game with President Eisenhower.

Probably because someone had dropped out – I was never told – late one afternoon I received a call from the White House saying the President would like for me to join them at Burning Tree at 11 o'clock the next morning. I accepted.

My then new boss was out of town. It was late in the day and after telling my secretary to cancel any appointments for the next day, I instructed her to say I had been called out of town for the day. I did not want her to say I had gone to Washington to play golf with the President and Fleck.

The next day I left home before dawn and drove to Washington. Along about Philadelphia I ran into heavy rain but kept on. Maybe this would be another day when "it never rains on a golf course." It wasn't.

The security guard had my name on his list and I was permitted to enter the Burning Tree clubhouse. When I walked in, Max Elbin, the head pro, said "You didn't get the message, did you?"

I had received no message that day as I had been on the road since 4 o'clock.

"This rain started last night and this morning we got word from the White House that today's plans were out. They were going to try to reach you before you left," Elbin added.

They had called but I was 200 miles down the road.

My sin, my "insubordination," dredged up months later was that I had – without notifying my boss – been out of my office on a day when he called a meeting.

Many firms would have taken pride that an employee answered a command appearance with the nation's chief executive.

Murrow assisted in getting that odious word off my record and it was replaced by the antiseptic "structural reorganization." I always took that to mean "you're fired" and a great many of the technicians and others who knew resented the action.

Those who were now working for Chirkinian were careful not to show their support by being too friendly. It didn't bother me that much. I had been hired to broadcast the PGA, not to stir up sympathy for what had been an embarrassing experience.

When Chirkinian made the announcer location assignments, I had expected to do the 18th hole since I was considerably more experienced in golf than the other announcers. Jim McKay was put in the booth at 18 and I was assigned to a platform in a tree – that's true. They built a place in a bushy tree for my observation tower of the action at the 16th hole.

My hole was an innocuous par three, maybe 160 yards long. It was about as challenging as a piece of cherry pie and I think it might have been a cherry tree I shared with the birds.

Rehearsals went remarkably well. I voiced the play of one group, otherwise relaxing at my perch among the limbs.

Just across an internal roadway was the

green of the 15th hole, a par five which was reachable in two by the longer hitters. Aware that Snead was having a good final round and would be likely to birdie, if not eagle, the 15th. I watched my monitor to see his group tee off on the 15th.

At that moment McKay switched to me to describe action at the short 16th. The players on the tee were not in the chase at this point. It had been some minutes since we had reported any action at 16, justifiably so.

After this group struck their tee shots, I remarked that while this trio played 16, the excitement was building at 15 to see if Snead could threaten Dow Finsterwald and Billy Casper by clipping one or two strokes off par at the hole across the road.

The intercom crackled. "You are to describe the 16th hole and forget about what's happening at 15. I know where I want the cameras to go. I'm calling the shots. Now be quiet."

That was lovable Frank, putting me in my place.

And then I was quiet.

Snead did not pick up any strokes at 15. In fact, he may have bogeyed it. Play continued and now the last group reached the 16th tee. McKay cued me to pick up the action by saying "and now to John Derr at 16..."

I said nothing. I'd been told to be quiet.

McKay... "and now let's bring in John Derr from the 16th..."

Silence.

Finally Jim said... "John Derr was in a tree at the 16th hole but he must have fallen out of the tree. I hope you're all right, John."

And Jim carried through to the end of the broadcast.

I packed up my pencils and pads and the binoculars which had never been taken from their case and climbed down from the tree. I walked directly to the parking lot, got in my car and headed north to Maine.

Until now Chirkinian never knew I heard all of his instructions, voice by McKay. I had never worked with Frank and didn't know his screams were impersonal and not intended to destroy and humiliate the subject...no matter who.

That was our first Difference Of Opinion. There would be others but I learned to respect Frank's judgment and opinion. I was wrong to ignore his commands at Llanerch. He made me a better broadcaster, just as he did with every reporter who worked under his command, doing it his way.

Now, regarding the April morning in Greensboro in 1969 when Chirkinian again said to me, "I'm calling the shots. You are going to the hospital." He was and I went.

The night before I had emceed a dinner meeting of the Carolinas Golf Reporters Association. It had been an enjoyable evening, a bountiful spread and a visit with old friends.

Among the delicacies offered were Carolina shrimp and since I had skipped lunch to play golf at Willow Creek I pigged it up on the shrimp. It was an early evening.

Back at the motel I checked through my notes for the broadcast and drifted off to sleep before midnight.

Around 6 A.M. I was awakened by severe stomach pain and regretted I'd eaten so many shrimp. I wondered if they might have been tainted.

The pain continued and I began to think maybe I was hungry for something other than seafood. Yes, I was just hungry. Up and dressed I went downstairs, crossed by the pool to the restaurant where I ordered scrambled eggs. They looked good but tasted awful. That was not the cure. By now I had begun to perspire heavily so I mopped my forehead, paid my check and started back to my room.

As we met, near the pool, Ray Scott expressed surprise that I was up so early and I told him why. "You don't look well. Let me take you back to your room."

Despite my assurances that the stomach pains were no big deal, Scott walked me back up the stairs to my room but I did successfully resist his offer to call a doctor.

Scott went straight to Chirkinian's room, awakened him and reported his concern. Together they came back to my room. By this time I was no longer perspiring...I was sweating.

"We're going to get you to the hospital," Frank said in his commanding voice that did not encourage any other opinion.

"No, Frank. There's no need for that. I'll be okay after I rest a while. Too many shrimp have upset my stomach."

"You are going to the hospital – now. On this show I'm calling the shots."

An ambulance was called and despite the fact a new recruit slipped on the wet steps and almost tilted me off the stretcher, we arrived at Cone Hospital. Frank was still in charge.

Emergency room personnel confirmed what Frank had suspected. It was a heart attack. I was placed in the Coronary Care Unit.

Several hours of relaxation while being monitored caused me to feel ready to go again. Although it had been diagnosed as a minor heart attack, I had my doubts. I denied it to myself, thinking it surely must have been only indigestion.

Rehearsal was scheduled for 3 o'clock and I wanted to be there. One doctor was almost convinced I could be released after lunch but he said the rehearsal was out. Meanwhile the CCU nurse, Nancy Fulton, cited some irregular readings on the instruments and the doctor was less confident I could leave.

Frank came back to the hospital about noon and was told I should be okay for the Saturday broadcast but no Friday rehearsal. Then Nurse Fulton took Frank aside for an explanation of what the readings meant.

At 1:17 P.M., while feeling quite well, the massive attack occurred. Sharper pains came back, the sweating resumed and I knew all was not well. Soaked with sweat, my gown was removed and I was wrapped in sheets. People were moving around me fast and then – suddenly I felt no pain – none at all.

This was the beginning of the near-death, after-death near-death syndrome. There was a finality about the way I felt. It did not seem to be a temporary thing. How long it lasted I don't know. I was aware of people around the bed but they faded away. Standing beside me – for I was no longer in bed – was my father who had been dead 28 years. I talked with him and others who had departed.

There was no consciousness of time.

As though awakening from a deep sleep, once again I was on the hospital bed. Unlike the hectic earlier action, those around me now spoke with calm, confident assurances that I was going to be all right.

And I was. This second attack at 1:17 had

been a doozy.

The damage to the left ventricle of my heart was severe and permanent. The scars that remain excite nurses and doctors who are seeing my EKG's for the first time.

After seven restricted weeks, no visitors, I was able to leave the hospital. In another month I was back on the TV tower. For my return Chirkinian hired a fork-lift tractor to hoist me topside and a Captain's chair to sit in. He overdid it when he hired two uniformed officers to escort me through crowds.

Frank was still "calling the shots."

With regard to the "out of body experience" it was all very clear and real to me at the time. I remembered it but vowed never to mention it to a soul for fear someone would accuse me of making it up.

About three years later, while on a multi-hour drive to Maine, I decided to speak about it to you but with the understanding it would not be repeated, lest someone think me daffy.

It was only a month or so later that you called one night and said, "Daddy, you know that story you told me about being out of your body when you had the second heart attack. Get the latest issue of Reader's Digest. There's an article in there that describes almost identically the experience you had."

So it did. I wasn't dreaming after all.

Four years after the attack I learned more about what went on that day. While having dinner with the doctor in whose care I was at Cone Hospital, I learned he had been elsewhere in the building when he heard the "Code Blue" call for emergency help. When he arrived at my room other doctors who answered sooner had told the nurses to pull the sheet over me. There were no life signs.

All efforts at getting a heart beat had failed and it looked as though the gig was up. Nurse Fulton asked if, as a last resort, she could try sternum massage. This is now known as CPR, cardio pulmonary resuscitation. Eureka, it worked.

A heartbeat activated the monitors and as the doctors and nurses watched in amazement the rhythmic beat continued. I was back among the living, at least for the moment.

The actual resuscitation had come through the hands of CCU Nurse Fulton but without the "don't argue with me" call by Chirkinian back at the motel six hours earlier it would not have been possible.

In a career that earned him awards and honors, Chirkinian made a million calls – calls to take camera three, get close on the ball, go to the scoreboard, next is a commercial.

For me his best call was that April morning when he said "You're going to the hospital. I'm calling the shots on this show."

"The Decision Maker"

Making decisions was a way of life for Joseph C. Dey. The former Philadelphia sports writer who, from his Executive Director desk, ran the United States Golf Association for three decades and then crossed over to become the first Commissioner of the PGA Tour, earned his moniker of "Mr. Golf."

If you've ever swung at a ball you were influenced by a Joe Dey decision. He was a longtime member of the committee that studied, modified and re-wrote the Rules of Golf used by the USGA and the Royal and Ancient of St. Andrews. And that means whenever golf is played, throughout the world.

I was never a victim of the Dey decisions on the course, but he figured prominently in three decisions that had an effect on my life and my career.

The USGA offices were in a mid-Manhattan brownstone former dwelling when I came to work at CBS.

Red Barber initiated a new radio sports program and one feature of it was to be a two to three minute unusual sports story to close each day's broadcast. Barber would do the baseball and football, Lou Effrat the boxing and track, Joe Palmer the horse racing, and I was to research tennis and golf.

It was for that purpose I went to the USGA offices and first met Joe Dey. I found him to be reservedly friendly, dressed in his Brooks Brothers suit and wearing a ceremonial tie. As a former sports writer he understood the type material I sought.

"I'm glad you are giving golf a prominence alongside those other sports," he told me. "I can help you find some interesting historic golf items that will serve your purpose."

It may be difficult to comprehend today, but in the mid-forties golf was seldom mentioned on radio, except the major tournaments. As a golf executive, Joe welcomed golf's inclusion in radio news.

We went into another small room. The entire USGA office consisted of three converted bedrooms. There on a dozen shelves was the USGA golf library, some old, a few new, but not too many.

"Do you know that a competitor in the British Open once almost had two consecutive holes-in-one?"

Without waiting for my negative reply, he reached for a red book and quickly found the story. It was precisely the type information I was seeking for a closing item.

In case you want to know who and when, it was Jock Hutchison in the 1921 Open at St. Andrews in the first round. He aced the eighth hole and with a favoring wind from the North Sea his drive on the 300 yard ninth carried straight toward the green.

As it was bounding along, an excited spectator rushed out and removed the flagstick. The ball was losing speed as it bumped up to and directly over the hole. Those at the green who saw it, swore that if the flagstick had remained in place, as it should have, Hutchison's ball would have tumbled into the hole for a second successive hole-in-one.

There were other details but that was the gist of the story. Red liked it and thus began my assignment of searching for other golf items. This influenced Barber to designate golf as my forte, and subsequently for CBS and other networks, I broadcast 185 live tournaments at home and abroad.

Dey's decision to provide me with the Hutchison story was pivotal to my researching and writing golf snippets. I must have written 100 of these for the Barber show but none more significant than that first one.

In 195o, the US Open was played at the Merion Cricket Club in Philadelphia. NBC purchased the broadcast rights for radio and their fledgling television network. Neither had a sponsor but NBC paid $10,000 for the rights, hoping to sell some commercial time.

Since it was unsponsored and NBC was to broadcast it as a news event, I appealed to Joe Dey to let CBS broadcast it also, as a news event. Petition denied.

The USGA director did agree to furnish our

reporters with "media" badges that would permit them to come on the grounds to observe play. We could not bring microphones on the course.

Bill Campbell, an able young broadcaster at WCAU, the CBS outlet in Philadelphia, shared my disappointment of denial but came up with a marvelous suggestion as a solution.

A local restaurant owner friend of his had a home just across the street from the14th fairway. In his front yard were half a dozen huge oak trees, old, tall and sturdy. He gave Campbell permission to build me a platform about 20 feet up in the tree, overlooking the course. From that perilous perch I could see parts of four holes, including the 18th green.

NBC set up its cameras on the course, covering the last three holes, the ones I could see visually.

Saturday morning I bought extra flight insurance and climbed the tree. Earle Janes was my engineer and he placed his equipment on the ground at the base of the tree. He ran the mike and cue lines up and taped them to a limb.

Throughout Saturday morning Campbell and his colleagues from WCAU observed play, and brought back third round reports to the tree. I had a string with one end tied to the tree and the other hanging loose on the ground. A clothes-pin attached to the loose end was where my leg men brought their reports and then I pulled up the string to get the updates.

Saturday afternoon on radio was usually filled with band music from Frank Dailey's Meadowbrook in New Jersey or a ballroom in Chicago. When I had a new report I asked Earle to call CBS Master Control in New York and tell them I needed the air for three minutes. If I ran over it didn't matter, they would just shorten the next song.

Meanwhile NBC was carrying the television to a few stations on the East coast and we were going across the country.

George Fazio came in with 287 and took the lead. He agreed to walk across the road for an interview and I came down from the tree to talk with George about his round. Before he left me, word came that Lloyd Mangrum had also come in with a 287.

Now only the exhausted recuperating Ben Hogan had a chance to tie or better their scores. He had three holes to play and we got word from inside the house that NBC had signed off, ended its coverage to switch to the commercial news programs.

When Hogan parred the 17th he now needed only another par at 18 to join the tie. I asked Master Control to let me have the network until Hogan finished, since we were the only ones on the air.

Hogan two-putted for his par and 287, making it a three-way tie with a playoff coming on Sunday at 18 holes. CBS Radio went back to music and we all felt good about our reporting the tie after NBC signed off.

Tuesday morning there was an urgent call from Joe Dey.

"I thought you understood NBC had bought the exclusive on-course coverage of the Open. Now I'm told you did play-by-play from the course on the last three holes," Dey stated.

"I beg to disagree, Joe. We abided by your rules."

"You did not broadcast on the course?"

"No, sir. I did frequent updates all afternoon and did report on Hogan's tie with Fazio and Mangrum, but I did all of my reports from the old oak tree."

"Will you write that in a letter to me today?"

"Certainly," I replied, "but why do you need it?"

"I need to show that to NBC. They claim I let you work on the course. They want their $10,000 check returned.

This time it was my decision to abide by Joe's edict that saved him the rights fee and we were both glad I did.

Dey voiced one other decision that had a profound effect on my life's work. Robert Trent Jones, my Montclair neighbor, had built an outstanding golf course in Montego Bay, Jamaica.

It was Half-Moon Rose Hall, four miles east of Montego.

The Jamaica Tourist Board wanted to use this as the focal point of a post-holiday pro-am tournament in early January. Visitors were in short supply the week after New Years and a golf tournament might fill a couple of hundred rooms.

Their first need was to find an organizer who was known to American golfers who could persuade clubs to send teams. There was a talented and successful amateur, who had won titles on both coasts, who seemed to fill the bill, but after going to Jamaica and studying the situation, he learned that if he accepted the paid position of director, based on his golfing achievements he would forfeit his amateur status.

He withdrew. Amateur ranking meant more than a job.

The search resumed and one day Trent asked me to join him and Joe Dey and John Pringle, the Jamaican Minister of Tourism, at a New York club to hear about their search for a director.

Pringle outlined his wants and they interested me. Jones gave me a great recommendation. Dey, at first, was more hesitant. He remarked that while I had never organized a tournament I had seen hundreds and was aware of the mistakes I should avoid.

Time for a decision. Pringle, knowing how his previous choice had bowed out at the last minute so he wouldn't lose his amateur standing, turned to Dey and said, "Well, what about Derr's status as an amateur?"

"No problem. He's not good enough to be an amateur."

Dey's decision to pass judgment on my playing ability and the unlikelihood that I would ever be good enough to be concerned about amateur status was a stunner. I may have been the only golfer he ever rated below amateur status.

But it was a decision with which I happily agreed and it opened the door to permit our family to spend part of 15 winters roaming the fairways and soaking up the sun on the beaches of Jamaica.

Not good enough? He was right, mon.

In New Delhi, India, during WWII there were published literally dozens of newspapers, all politically oriented. The only newsy daily, *The Statesman,* was also the only one printed in English.

It was in their print shop that was published the Theater newspaper, the *China-Burma-India Roundup,* of which I was the sports editor. Every Thursday our GI staff spent the afternoon at *The Statesman,* reading proof, supervising layout and going to press with the 16-page edition of stateside news and commentary.

Through this we came to know many of the staff members of *The Statesman.* One was an Indian reporter, Devadas Gandhi, who often came to the composing room to visit us. He had a great interest in how we put together our paper and contrasted it with their methods.

Devadas and I became good friends and one day he asked if I would like to go with him to meet his father. "Of course," I replied, not too excitedly, but courteously. Gandhi is a very common name in India and originally meant shopkeeper or merchant.

About three weeks later I was startled to learn that the father of Devadas Gandhi was Mohandas, known affectionately as the Mahatma.

That Thursday when Devadas came to the

composing room, I sheepishly apologized for my seeming indifference to his invitation to meet his father. "I would greatly appreciate meeting your father," I told him. And the next week, Devadas, who was about 40 years old, and I climbed on our bicycles and peddled three miles to Old Delhi, where his father lived in a neat small rented home.

When we entered what I took to be his living room, I was tingling with excitement. To see sitting cross-legged on the floor, drawn up to a small square table little larger, but about as high as a footstool...the Mahatma himself. A nervousness I had seldom known engulfed me.

We had interrupted the old man writing, using a quill and ink on unruled paper. He placed the quill in a glass holder by the inkwell and looked up as Devadas said: "This is my American friend I told you about."

I bent forward to shake his extended hand and he motioned for me to take a seat on the floor beside him. Devadas sat first on his right and I followed him.

Tea was offered and although I did not usually drink tea at 4:00 in the afternoon I accepted and sipped.

I had looked forward to meeting this powerful religious and political leader, but had never considered what I could or should say conversationally.

Mr. Gandhi rescued me from my silence. He asked where in America I lived, what had been my employment, and what was my father's profession.

I was to learn that Mr. Gandhi was not an idle talker and in his presence I felt an unusual desire to listen rather than to chit-chat. He had once written that "a man of few words will rarely be thoughtless in speech. He will measure every word. We find so many people impatient to talk. All this talking can hardly be...of any benefit to the world. It is so much a waste of time."

After that initial visit I looked forward to my returns with Devadas to have tea with the Mahatma. And in time I was more comfortable in carrying on a conversation, although the subject was neither politics nor religion.

Getting to know him in this manner piqued my interest in his career, of which I was only superficially aware. I visited every Hindu bookstore in New Delhi and bought every book of his or about him that I could find.

His goal at that time was to assure the peoples of India that they would be freed from British rule as soon as the war was won. Several times past he had thought he had such an understanding, but India remained a servitude sector of the British Empire.

The Japanese made threatening gestures to involve India on the side of the Axis. Gandhi had warned Japan to keep its distance. He relied on finally getting out from under British domination and he saw no advantage in becoming equally deprived under imperial Japanese rule.

In 1944 Gandhi met with Gen. Sir Archibald Wavell, then Viceroy of India, in a three-weeks peace conference in the summer capital of Simla. I was ordered to wear my War Correspondent uniform and monitor the press briefings, but not to write about them in our Theater paper. Instead I was to observe, inquire and discover, using my own initiative, what the British were offering and what the Indians were requesting.

This information was to be relayed to Washington.

It was no mistake to have been sent on this assignment. I knew not only Gandhi, but also was friendly with Jawaharlal Nehru, his Hindu lieutenant, with whom I frequently shared coffee in the India Coffee House in New Delhi.

Lord Wavell had been an excellent golfer and often played the Delhi course with Johnny Goodman, former USGA Open and Amateur champion. Goodman had introduced me to the Viceroy at the golf club and I had been invited by his staff to several dances at the Vice-Regal Lodge in Old Delhi.

Peace sessions followed the pattern of several hours of talking, a press briefing and then two days to counsel with their group before the next session. It was no problem for me to use those two days to visit with staff and try to learn the next move.

It would be pleasing to say that Gandhi's meetings there set the stage for India's liberation, but not so. He and Wavell were in accord, but before the war ended a new government took power in England and the whole process had to be started over.

Gandhi wanted India to be home to both the Moslem and Hindu faiths but eventually it was divided into two countries, India and Pakistan, and has been in turmoil ever since.

Sergeants do not talk political policy with world leaders of the statue of Gandhi, a man whom Gen. George C. Marshall described as "the spokesman for the conscience of all mankind." Even so, in the perhaps 20 private sessions I spent with him, some of his beliefs filtered into the conversation.

India was an extremely poor country and had been for decades, maybe even centuries. And with the preponderance of beggars it was inevitable that the subject of poverty and how countries could confront it would come up.

There was a conversation dealing with this one particular evening I recall. Because I did not take notes and thus cannot solely rely upon my recollection, I quote from a magazine article written by Gandhi in 1925:

"If I had the power, I would stop every donation where free meals are given. It has degraded the nation and it has encouraged laziness, idleness, hypocrisy and even crime.

"Such misplaced charity adds nothing to the wealth of the country...and gives a false sense of meritoriousness to the donor. How nice and wise it would be if the donor were to open institutions where they would give meals under healthy, clean surroundings to men and women who would work for them...The rule should be: 'No labor, no meal.'

"It will be cheaper in the long run, if we do not want to increase the race of loafers which is fast overrunning this land."

That was written by Gandhi in 1925.

Gandhi was a remarkable man. His own modesty was a sterling trait. I consider myself fortunate to have had this experience with Mahatma.

I'm glad Devadas took me to meet his father.

The trans-Atlantic call came to me in my room at London's Cumberland Hotel just before the dinner hour.

When I answered, the operator said: "Please hold for a call from New York."

CBS was calling. News Director Ted Church said he had bad news and good news. "Red Barber is in intensive care in a Pittsburgh hospital. He was playing golf at the Pittsburgh Field Club today when an ulcer blew out on him. He nearly died from loss of blood but they got him to the hospital and he's doing okay now.

"That's the bad news. He will not be coming to London to broadcast the Olympics. The good news is we want you to take over and anchor our Olympic coverage. Howard K. Smith, who is stationed here in London, can help you. And we are sending David Schoenburn from the CBS Paris bureau, and we'll have a stringer named Stephen Laird for whatever use you want for him.

"You will follow the broadcast schedule that Red was to do. Remember, in addition to your quarter-hour reports, we will want updates on the CBS World News Roundup and Ed Murrow wants you to do two minutes every night on his show."

My head was spinning, my heart was pounding and I had trouble accepting the immensity of the assignment. I had come to

London as a writer/producer and never aired one word over the CBS Radio network.

I wondered...was my close friend and boss, Red Barber, really recovering...was I up to taking over for him...was I ready to begin my CBS broadcast career describing the opening of the 1948 Olympics...was anyone ever so fortunate to be in the right place at the right time and deserving of such confidence from one's peers? I wondered.

There was no time to get nervous or doubt that the assignment could be carried off as requested.

My wife, Peggy, and I had crossed the Atlantic on the SS America with the full contingent of Olympic athletes and officials. This had given us five days at sea to get to know many of the competitors and coaches, a fact that stood us in great stead.

Peggy had formerly worked at NBC in New York and was knowledgeable about much of the backstage planning that would be necessary. She took over some of my production duties and also served as a reporter of events such as basketball, boxing and swimming.

I checked the vast schedule of events to see which ones I might report personally and others were assigned to cover those I had to pass up due to being on the air. Smith arranged for me to do the early news shows from BBC Broadcast House in Center City and the others I did from Wembley

Stadium's broadcast enclave. Reporters by the hundreds shared this space and the gibberish going around the world intrigued me.

In 48 hours the white doves of peace would be released and circle over the crowded stadium, at one end of which smoke rose from the eternal Olympic flame.

So much to do in so little time.

Early on opening day, ticketed for a spot in the broadcast area, we arrived at Wembley Stadium. The first two locations to which we were directed proved not to be the correct ones.

Then a helpful usher, only slightly less confused than I, correctly interpreted my tickets and led us – the BBC technician, Peggy and me – up several flights of stairs and pointed to an area in an already overcrowded section.

More helpful ushers cleared our spaces, which had been mistakenly occupied by some other foreigners whose language I could not identify but who spoke in unkind tomes about being asked to vacate the CBS location.

We awaited the big moment.

One level below us, directly beneath our perch, there was a large section devoid of spectators. But not for long.

There was an explosion of enervated excitement as King George VI led the procession of the ruling family into the Royal Box. There came the Queen, followed by Princess Elizabeth, who within four years would become Queen Elizabeth II. Prince Phillip and others came in, to much applause.

We should have known those empty seats were for some important people. Of the thousands of seats in Wembley, these were the only ones with padded cushions.

What a moment to remember. Just in front and below us sat the entire Royal family. And I liked my seats better, up higher.

Time. How much time until they start. CBS had agreed to carry the opening live and I hoped they would be on time as I debuted on CBS. Yes, they are on time. The stadium announcer spoke and then King George VI was heard to say: "I declare open the 1948 Olympics." Not a long speech but he did it well.

At that signal the 5,000 white doves were released from their cages and in an ever widening circle flew over London.

The first broadcast was on its way and in the next three weeks 73 more followed. I had "taken over" as requested and was trying my best to paint for the American public the tapestry of the 1948 Olympics...but I was no Red Barber, the best.

To have made the opening ceremony of the 1948 London Olympics my first broadcast for CBS radio was an event of unscripted attainment. Lucky again.

Sir Clifford Campbell, a large, friendly man with the demeanor of a school teacher, which he was before he became the Governor-General, sat on my left on the dais as we prepared to distribute the prizes that had been won in another Jamaica Jamboree. Behind those big round glasses, Sir Clifford's eyes twinkled with a laughing mode that defined satisfaction.

As is the custom in Jamaica, and I suppose in all countries that have an allegiance to the British crown, the evening's festivities begin with the toast to the Queen. This we did promptly since protocol does not permit smoking until after the toast, and this was in the days when dinner smoking was permitted.

Next it was time to introduce Sir Clifford and let him extend greetings to the 200 golfers and wives who had been in his country 10 or 12 days competing in our annual invitational pro-am. He did this nicely. He had the experience. But he did one other thing that attracted my attention.

Most of the golfers were from the United States, but teams were chosen from Canada, England, Scotland, Ireland, France and Spain, and one year we had a team from Budapest that included Charlie Chaplin's son.

Even so, the Gov.-General always paid tribute to the sitting President of the United States and this is not usually the case in a foreign country if no representative of the State Department is present. Sir Clifford did it every year, with warmth and grace.

I was so impressed with this that one year I wrote to President Nixon and asked if there was any reply I should make in his behalf.

During the week before Christmas my daughter was hosting a 4-H Club holiday party at my home and the house was full of high-spirited youngsters. The phone rang and although it might be some mother calling to tell her daughter she was en route to pick her up, I quickly answered. And I was glad I did.

The operator said: "Please hold for the White House."

I could only imagine the reply that this might have evoked. After confirming this was the right number, Rosemary Woods, personal secretary to Mr. Nixon, came on the line.

After exchanging holiday small talk with me, Rosemary said the President asked her to call and instruct me to tell the Gov.-General how much he personally appreciated the good wishes for himself and our country. This was at a time when many foreign governments were shooting darts instead of kudos.

"I would have written you a letter from the President, but with the mails so delayed this time of year I thought it best to call you because the President is most anxious for you to deliver his message," she said.

At the dinner, after the Jamaican leader's welcome and again a tribute to the President, I was able to say on behalf of the President his gesture of friendship was most appreciated.

The dinner proceeded. Midway through the second course, Sir Clifford leaned over and asked me to introduce him again. I had emceed many dinners but could not recall introducing the same person to the same audience twice at one sitting.

At a convenient time I arose, cleared my throat and asked if the audience would direct their attention to the dais as we were going to have another word from the Gov.-General.

Sir Clifford, seeing nothing unusual in this, then spoke these words: "On behalf of Her Majesty, the Queen, it is my privilege to confer full Jamaican citizenship on Mr. and Mrs. Derr and their daughter, Cricket."

Flabbergasted at this unexpected development, my immediate response to Sir Clifford was... "Do I get to vote, or do I have to pay taxes?"

There was a purpose, I later learned. This was during the Cuban crisis, when planes were occasionally hijacked over Cuba. The American Embassy was closed, but the Jamaican Embassy was open, and since we made this flight often there was a chance we might be apprehended. Sir Clifford wanted it so we could request to be taken to the Jamaican Embassy and repatriated immediately.

Never used...but the news revealed by the re-introduction was reassuring on Caribbean flights.

It was a crystal clear late summer Sunday and fans who had flocked to the Robinson Country Club course without head gear felt the heat. There was no wind, no shadeless relief.

Now reverberating over the hilly Illinois countryside was a voice that, when modulated to a whisper, had the timbre of Moses reading the Ten Commandments...and was just as dynamic. When heard from the rostrum of the United States Senate it needed no microphone. Nor did it today. But it had one, the little desk mike that sat on a makeshift table in front of us.

Everett McKinley Dirksen was a veteran Senator from the Land of Lincoln. He was not running for president but I always thought he would have made a good one. Instead he was making one last run to return again to the Senate and some of his Democrat foes were claiming he was too old, out of touch.

Some things never change, notice.

At any rate, his handlers felt some of this "too old" chatter could be silenced if Dirksen was seen to be active in sports matters. With the polls showing he could use a boost it was decided he should expose an identity with the younger sports fans at a golf tournament.

Dick Heath, whose Heath candy bars were made there in Robinson, invited Senator Dirksen to come see some of the Sunday round and he was to be a guest commentator with me at the long par four 17th hole, from which I anchored the broadcast.

Asking the Senator to make the customary and somewhat uncomfortable climb up the ladder to our platform was out of the question. He must have a more dignified ascent.

Thursday morning a covey of carpenters and three truckloads of lumber arrived at 17 and they constructed a platform that looked like one side of the Egyptian pyramids. It started out very wide and narrowed as it rose toward the heavens.

At about 20 feet it flattened out and the platform was enclosed by railings. We had never had one so roomy, never one so easy to mount, never one with such comfortable chairs.

About noon, a couple of hours before the broadcast, word came to me that the Senator had arrived and I should come meet him. He was a most impressive man, huge hands and that rumbling voice which was his trademark as an orator.

An aide said he understood I was staying in one of the club cottages on the grounds and asked if I would object to taking Mr. Dirksen there to let him lie down and relax a spell.

Not at all.

We walked the 200 yards to the cottage and I told him how much I admired his powerful presentation of his point of view. It interested me because I did a little public speaking myself.

"I'm on a tour of five Midwest colleges where I'll give my talk this week," I proudly told the Senator.

"What do you talk about, sports?"

"Yes, but more than sports," I told him. "I have a talk the educators seem to like. It has to do with urging people to do the best they can, even if they are not the best, because not every one can be No. 1. I call it: "The Importance of Imperfection.""

By now we had reached the cottage. "That's a great title and sounds like an interesting subject. Have you published it? I have connections with Reader's Digest and possibly can have it published."

"No, I'd rather not. The schools pay me $800 to make this speech and if I publish it I'll have to get another subject."

Dirksen now had his shoes off and stretched out on the bed. "Maybe you could let me hear you give the talk."

This was pretty heady stuff. Dirksen was acclaimed as our most distinguished orator...and he wanted to hear my talk.

As though on the stage, I began.

In less than a minute, I heard the resonate snoring. So much for my chance to impress the silver-throat of the Senate.

Move forward now to late afternoon. The broadcast was going well and only a few more leading groups were to come to the 17th. Still no Dirksen. Then I saw the officers and staffers bringing him up the walk and he made the easy climb up to our platform.

"What a perfectly lovely place to watch the play. This looks so easy from up here."

"Senator, do you play golf?"

"No. I don't have time for it anymore. I used to play and I enjoyed it. I have a wonderful set of clubs, maybe 25 or 30, sitting in a closet in Washington, gathering dust."

As the threesome came up our fairway, I explained the absolute necessity of being quiet when players were close by.

"Oh, yes, I can see that this might disturb them."

His understanding eased my mind.

Then came the next group and a contender in it was a Washington boy who had only recently turned professional – a short, stocky fellow named Deane Beman.

"This young man is from your town, Senator. He is Deane Beman. I'm sure you've seen his name in the papers."

"Oh, yes. And isn't it wonderful that all these

people have come out here today to see him."

I let that pass and reminded him we must be quiet.

Dirksen nodded but had sympathy for Beman and the four-foot putt he needed to make for his par and he volunteered the thought... "As close as that is, don't you think they should give it to him?"

Beman backed off, glanced our way and started over.

Again he was set. I had reached over and covered Dirksen's mike with my hand, a sign for silence.

"Do you think he can hear us now?"

Beman looked up again and walked away.

"Senator, he may not hear you but he will think he can if he sees your lips moving, so we MUST NOT TALK."

Beman made the putt and I removed my choke hold on Dirksen.

Later Beman told me he hadn't missed a word of Dirksen's from the time he crossed the creek 210 yards away. "One more word from that tower and you'd have been ducking a putter."

Yes, Senator, golfers think they hear worms breathe.

The late November skies were laden gray but it was still too pretty a day in Princeton to turn down an invitation to play golf. Earlier in the day it had been my duty to check out the CBS Radio facilities at Palmer stadium, where on Saturday Dartmouth would challenge Princeton for the Ivy League title.

Mack Morris, an advertising executive who lived near the stadium, suggested we bundle up and go for a fast round.

On the 14th hole, the sun having moved much lower in the sky, we drove and more briskly started our walk up the fairway.

Coming in our direction was a lone figure, out for a walk no doubt, with a heavy scarf around his head. He wore an overcoat that was long enough to have been issued by the Cossacks.

"Do you know who that is?" asked Mack.

I had no idea.

"That's Albert Einstein," he told me. "He walks out here almost every day. Would you like to meet him?

Einstein? Who wouldn't like to meet Einstein?

We altered our path and diagonally cut across the fairway to intersect with Mr. Einstein, now recognizable as enough of that bumper crop of white hair extended out from under his scarf to serve as identification, looking just like his pictures.

Mack introduced us and I felt somewhat flabbergasted, standing in the middle of the 14th fairway, talking with the great scientist. Here he was, maybe the only man in the world who understood his theory of relativity.

"Mr. Einstein," I asked, "do you play golf?"

For just a moment he seemed to hesitate and I wondered if he had heard my question. Then, in that deep guttural mid-European accent, he answered. He looked at me and almost apologetically said:

"Tried it once. Couldn't understand it. Quit."

And you wonder why you can't understand this game. If a brain like Einstein couldn't ...well.

About three miles west of New Delhi lay the Royal Gymkhana Golf Club, the clubhouse being an abandoned red brick mosque sitting in a grove of small trees. The parking lot is small but the bicycle racks extend for 50 feet. Gas rationing encouraged peddling to the links.

The course is an attractive 18-hole layout with small greens and basically rather flat. There are no water holes but there is one memorable hole, known as the Monkey Hole. The par-three is 155 yards across a deep heavily vegetated chasm.

The tee sits on the edge of this chasm and across the way the green is at about the same elevation. But to reach it one must descend a steep winding path, then across the floor of the chasm and climb another steep winding path probably 80-90 feet to the green.

Families of monkeys live in the underbrush and caves about the course and it was not unusual to drive to an empty green only to see when you arrived that six or eight monkeys were cavorting on the green.

What they did with the balls they carried off in their mouths we never figured out. I'm sure they were not eaten but look as we did we never found their cache, which must have contained literally hundreds of balls. We suspected some caddie had found it and was selling back our lost monkey hole balls.

Eventually we learned to send a fore caddie ahead to shoo away the monkeys before we hit. Being protected by the tenets of Hinduism, one dared not harm the little rascals.

This hole, No. 7, stands out in my memory not only because of the monkeys but because it was a hole where I lost $100 bet. And there is a story that goes with that.

There was a sergeant from California with whom I played often and while our wagers were modest, a couple of rupees or so, Dave had a steady stream of losses to me.

There was a colonel from New York, Col. John R. Mott, who also played often with Dave and against him Dave seldom lost.

On other days, when Mott and I played, the victory almost always went to the colonel. He had my number. I could beat Dave, Dave could beat Mott and Mott could beat me. That happens a lot in golf.

Dave was clever with card games and every payday, by dawn every month he would have a big roll. One month, after a successful all-night card game, Dave was flush. He called and asked if we could play the next Thursday and he thought he had found a way to beat me.

He proposed a 36-hole match, just the two of us, for $100 per hole. That was high but since our matches usually were only a couple of holes up or down, I accepted.

At the appointed hour, each with a caddie and a fore-caddie, we set out. Luck was with me and I went one up at the first. And then the second and the next four. When we arrived at the monkey hole, No. 7, I had a six up advantage.

An errant tee shot into the chasm resulted in a double bogey and my first loss. Buoyed by his comeback, Dave swung hard, harder than usual, and hooked left into the brush on the next tee. Lost ball. He never recovered after No. 8.

The next 9 holes came to me and when we stopped for lunch my winnings were $1,600. All but the monkey hole. We tied No. 18.

Before we ate, Dave asked if he could call off the afternoon 18, which delighted me. With $1,600 in hand, why chance losing it and he was sure to get back on his game in the afternoon. Lunch for me tasted good.

When we finished Dave suggested we drop back to our usual wager and play an afternoon round, inasmuch as we were at the club and with nothing better to do.

We did. Dave lost, one down.

The monkey hole wasn't kind but the day was like a dream, even losing that one hole. A memorable day and hole.

Dave continued to beat the Colonel. The Colonel continued to beat me. And Dave and I seldom played after that day.

On the elongated tee of Carnoustie's elongated 16th hole, a par three of 235 yards with a green shaped like an upside down saucer, Ben Hogan's terse comment to me in the 1953 British Open remains the most memorable moment in my six decades of reporting golf.

He had just played his tee shot and when it rolled to a stop some 12 feet below the cup, Hogan eased over to my side of the tee where I was standing. He waited a moment, lit a cigarette and watched Hector Thompson drive. Then he quietly turned to me and said, "John, you can go in and get ready for your broadcast. This tournament's over..."

There was no bravado in his matter-of-fact statement. Instead there was a look of casual intensity in his steel gray eyes. His was confident appraisal of the situation – unexpected, uncharacteristic, unmistakable. The soft tone of his voice, the laconic look on his face and the circumstance of place and time told me this was a special moment to remember.

Hogan was playing well. So far in this final round he was three under par, five under for the tournament. Coming down the 15th fairway, a few moments earlier, Hogan had beckoned me to join him inside the phalanx of six large Scottish policemen who helped him move through the crushing crowds from greens to tees and down the fairway.

The gallery had taken the American champion to its heart, as though he were a native son. He attracted huge crowds wherever he went, to practice, to putt or just walking to his car. Earlier in the week we devised a maneuver to stymie autograph-seekers. Hogan carried his putter in his right hand, making it unavailable for shaking hands or writing, and his left hand was hidden behind me, clutching the belt at the back of my trousers.

Knowing his penchant for total concentration and aware he was nursing a cold and a temperature of more than 100 degrees, on the first tee I had told Ben I would be close by but would not speak with him unless he called to me. I did not expect to be called, but was available.

There were no public scoreboards around the course but there were several way station tents in which R & A officials took shelter and maintained phone contact with the scoring. As a press representative, my badge let me in to ask questions.

By this time I knew Stranahan, Dai Rees and Peter Thompson had each finished at 286, two under par. Roberto de Vicenzo, with whom Hogan had been tied for the lead starting the last round, was doing poorly, now several over. Hogan was five under.

When Ben motioned for me to join him on the 15th, he must have heard how those ahead of him had done. "Where does Cerda stand? See if you can find out."

The Argentine, Antonio Cerda, had done 69 in the morning to be only one behind. If he was still hot he might be closing in or may even have the lead.

Off I scurried to check on Cerda. At the 15th green I gave Hogan the word that at 13 Cerda was three under. "Is he on the tee or green at 13?" Hogan asked. He parred 13 and remains three under, I reported.

Cerda was the last real challenger still on the course and Hogan had him by two strokes with three holes to play. Three holes, but what holes. They may have been the toughest last three holes in tournament golf at that time.

The 16th you know about. Both the 17th and 18th were long, not only long at 454 and 496, but the meandering Barry Burn, an innocent-looking but dangerous little stream, crossed each fairway twice.

The difficulty of those holes, with almost no chance to pick up a stroke except on the 18th, which was played as a par five at the time, plus the fact that despite leaving putt after putt just short, Hogan still by two, may have ignited the confidence he showed me at the 16th tee.

Cerda parred in. Hogan birdied 18 and won by four strokes.

As Hogan had known, my broadcast time

schedule was tight. He completed his round only eight minutes before my overseas phone lines were ordered to carry the broadcast back to CBS/New York and on across the country.

After signing his card, Hogan came with me to the Starter's Box, a small frame building by the first tee. The BBC technicians had converted this into our studio.

A brief overview of the tournament led us into Hogan's hole-by-hole recapitulation. We had covered the first six holes, with Ben telling me the clubs he had played, lengths of the putts and such, when I looked out the window and saw it was raining again. Here came Valerie Hogan, a plastic bonnet shielding her from the rain as she walked down from their rented car toward the ceremony stand, where the crowd had gathered.

I thought I should get her out of the rain.

After starting the description of the seventh hole, I walked out to invite Valerie inside. She refused, despite the weather. Valerie always shunned the spotlight or special treatment even when it meant staying dry.

Meanwhile I had left Hogan alone with a live microphone, recounting his play on the seventh. By the time I returned Hogan was describing a putt, a putt I remembered being on the eighth, not the seventh green.

Not until I heard the tape back in New York that next week was I aware that Hogan had concluded his comments about the seventh and said... "Well, John, on the 8th, I put the ball down the right side and..." What a pro he was... in all ways.

It rained during the presentation but I did not go out for the ceremony. Too many of my newly acquired "friends" of the British press were fuming because Hogan had gone with me instead of to the press tent. They thought, and some of them still write, that I kidnapped Hogan. No such thing.

Later I joined Ben in the locker room lounge and reminded him I had promised Joe Dey to bring back to the USGA museum the ball with which Hogan finished, regardless of place.

"Yes," Ben said. "Timmy (Cecil Timms, his caddie) has it in his pocket."

As I started out to find the caddie Hogan called to me, "Ask Timmy about the other ball too."

With his heavy coat shielding Hogan's clubs as the misty rain continued, Timmy stood just outside the door. I asked him for the winning ball for the USGA. He fetched it from his pocket.

"Mr. Hogan told me to ask you about the other one."

From another pocket Timmy brought out another ball. He handed me a 90 compression, English-size Titleist No. 2. "This is the ball we holed for a birdie deuce at the 12th hole. Mr. Hogan told me to save it. He said Mr. Derr might want it for a souvenir. That was our only deuce the last round."

My souvenir had been stored at the 16th tee, but I was pleased that the "wee Ice Mon" as the Scots called him had shown a warm, caring, sentimental side that few believed he possessed.

This closed out a remarkable week for me. After seeing Hogan win at Augusta in April, I started politicking my CBS bosses to let me cover the Open at Carnoustie. Then after he won the U.S. Open at Oakmont, I begged to have them send me.

There was no enthusiasm even though I all but promised them he was going to win on his first try at that event. Golf was not a big deal for the radio networks and television was a non-factor. Eventually I got the OK but without a commercial sponsor it would be an extremely low budget affair.

Air transportation was arranged through a barter swap with BOAC, but housing was a different matter. The CBS travel agent said there was only one first rate hotel in Carnoustie, the Bruce. It had been booked solid for weeks.

"There might be a cancellation," I pleaded and every day I begged them to keep on trying.

Four days before I was to fly over came the word that a room had opened up and I was booked at the Bruce. What a relief.

Then a strange coincidence. The Hogans had

booked a room at the Bruce Hotel as soon as Ben sent in his entry. When he arrived at the hotel, Hogan learned it had no rooms with private baths. Ben needed to soak his damaged legs in a hot tub each morning and that wouldn't be possible.

The Hogans checked out before they checked in and Ben accepted an invitation offered earlier to stay at the NCR house in Dundee, a few miles away. Hogan rented a car and moved there.

I would have appreciated a private bathroom myself but most of all I appreciated Hogan's bed. That was the cancellation. Although I had covered many of his victories, including his first at the Pinehurst No. 2 course in the 1940 North and South Open, I had never been what one might call close to Ben. Few writers were but perhaps because I was very friendly with Sam Snead, his undeclared personal adversary, I was less close than most.

When one is out of his own country, overseas, it seems the bond of being a fellow countryman overrides any differences. Friendships are easier made and more binding. Such was the case with Hogan at Carnoustie. He became my friend.

During two Hogan practice rounds, two qualifying rounds and the four championship rounds, I walked every step of the way with him until the 71st and 72nd holes.

If he played in the morning, we usually had lunch together, although he ruined my appetite for three days when he once told me the dish we had just eaten was lamb stew. I simply cannot, would not, knowingly, eat lamb in any fashion.

Those luncheons, after or before play, gave me a relaxed atmosphere in which to quietly ask Hogan questions, mostly about course strategy but occasionally a matter of technique. Many knew how he played. They could watch and see. I saw how he thought and it was the Hogan thinking process that made him great. There were better ball strikers, perhaps, but not better thinkers.

Speaking of technique, one day Hogan told me five things about striking a ball that I never read in his books. They were not necessarily applicable to every golfer but he thought those five moves would help correct errors in my swing. I jotted them down in my notebook as we sat at the table.

Afterwards he demonstrated these changes he recommended might be beneficial to me. He was careful not to say this was the only way golf should be taught, but these were major flaws he had noticed in my efforts on the practice tee. I never played a hole with him, otherwise he might have noticed 10 mistakes.

Three of his five suggestions were static, having to do with pre-swing placement of appendages – hands, feet, fingers, shoulders and head. One was weight dispersal. Only one actually had to do with motion. That surprised me, but I think he was saying that unless you are correct before you start to swing, nothing you do during the motion can produce the desired result.

"Don't write about these things. They might not be understood just by reading them. And don't ever tell anyone these five things because some might not apply to others. I'll let you know when you can write about them."

Had Hogan revealed "his secret" everyone talked about? It may have been in there and I was not smart enough to know.

I hoped he'd release the prohibition one day but that would be of no value now. I can't remember them exactly and I've lost my notes. Let's see, one of them was...

Carnoustie was a great experience.

Ben Hogan, my new friend, made it so.

Holding the news release in his hand, Edward R. Murrow walked into my CBS office one afternoon and asked a most unexpected question. "May I join your announcing crew at this golf tournament down in Virginia?"

Ed Murrow doing a golf tournament? Incredible.

He was America's most listened to and popular newscaster. But this was golf.

Without waiting for my question of why, the tall handsome reporter gave me the answer.

The tournament was called the Cavalier Specialist tournament and was the brainchild of Sidney Banks, owner of the Cavalier Hotel at Virginia Beach.

Two five-man teams of golf professionals had been chosen because of their specialty shots. Each team had one player to drive, one for second shots, another for chipping, one for trouble shots and the putters were Bobby Locke and Johnny Palmer.

Walter Hagen was captain of one team and Gene Sarazen the other. They could collaborate with their team and decide how and by whom each shot should be played.

But one wondered what was Murrow's interest other than seeing ten of the country's top players in this unique match.

Murrow explained. In 1937 he was in England, primarily as a talent scout for the CBS Public Affairs Department, arranging for foreign speakers and culture programs.

CBS Radio assigned him to go to Southport, England and cover the Ryder Cup golf matches between the USA and Great Britain. He was to broadcast a 15-minute summary at the conclusion of play.

The USA won and Murrow began to write his report. He had arranged for Hagen, the non-playing captain, and Sarazen, the captain, to join him in the attic of a nearby house where BBC had arranged for the broadcast to originate.

They climbed the stairs and Murrow took his place on one side of the table. Hagen and Sarazen sat across from him.

Murrow opened his report with the news that the USA had won by a score of 8 to 4. He then brought on his guests and they talked the three minutes he had allotted for interviews.

Murrow thanked them for appearing and reached across to shake hands before they departed. When Hagen extended his big mitt to shake he reached over and picked up Murrow's written report. Hagen and Sarazen headed for the door and Murrow reached for the panic button.

Since the broadcast was live and the only other person present was the BBC engineer who was interested only in his instrument needles and his stop watch, there was no one to help.

With Murrow's script in hand Hagen disappeared through the door, down the steps and probably back to the bar.

"For the next 12 minutes the American public heard the most colorful description of how green the grass grew on the golf course," Murrow said.

"I knew the USA had won but I could not recall the score of a single match, who had won and who had lost. So I talked on about the beauty of the golf course and how wonderful to spend a day in the English countryside.

"I think that may have been only the third broadcast I had done for CBS and I was helpless without my notes and script. Hagen thought it was a great joke.

"But that was then," laughed Murrow, who in the intervening years had done thousands of broadcasts, including his great series of wartime reports from London. "I've waited a long time to get even with Hagen and this is my chance."

Murrow would have been a bonus for us that day but a late assignment elsewhere denied him his revenge. That may have made their post Ryder Cup match: Hagen 1, Murrow 1.

[Another one I remember with pride]

"Don't Be Upset"

If they ever cancelled horse shows because of the heat and hot weather, the one in which you competed at the Little River Farms in July one summer would have been called off at dawn.

There had been no rain for days. The show ring was dusty, despite being heavily sprinkled overnight. By 10 o'clock the temperature had hit the century mark and was climbing.

This was a major show, a week-long event that had attracted riders and some expensive horses from a dozen or more states.

What I remember most, in addition to the heat, was your performance on Poco Jeep McCue, your registered gray quarterhorse in the Open Jumper class. This was a large class on the first round, only eight of the 27 cleared every jump.

When they raised the rails, those who failed to clear the jump were eliminated. Up higher they went. More failed.

You completed another clean ride and most of the field had competed. Then a young rider from Chicago also was perfect. This meant the two of you would be brought back for a jump-off.

Not only did they raise the rails but you would be racing against time as well. It would mean going all out the whole way.

While the workmen again re-set the hurdles, you came to the car, looking for me. You called me aside, so no one could hear our conversation.

"Don't be upset, Daddy, but I'm not going to punish Jeep in this hot weather by working him again. He's worked hard today, did everything I asked of him, but it's too hot now. Is it all right if I hold him out? Are you disappointed with my decision?"

I was disappointed. Jeep was clearing the jumps with room to spare, even after all those trips around the course. He and you were doing so well, I felt sure you could win the blue.

But at the same time I was proud of you.

Many riders, so close to victory, would have let their egos overrule reality, with no consideration for what further discomfort it would have been for their horse.

Your many local friends, awaiting the jump-off, were shocked and disappointed when you told the judge you and Jeep were retiring. They begged you to continue, confident you could bring home the victory. I thought so, too, but silently applauded your evaluation of priorities.

Some may have thought you got "cold feet" but a "warm heart" for your faithful horse that let the Illinois girl take home the blue ribbon.

Your love and regard for all animals is a trait you inherited from your mother. Pride replaced my disappointment.

Jeep and Cricket
who made me write these stories

"YOUR I.D., PLEASE?"

Like most celebrated or famous people, Arthur Godfrey was denied the privilege of freely moving about in public. When he did, sometimes the results were bizarre.

One day during lunch time, after he had eaten a luncheon salad at his desk, as he did most days, Arthur called and asked me if I would go with him on a short shopping tour over on Fifth Avenue.

Normally he would call for his car and drive or be driven, even on a short trip, three or four blocks, as this would be. It was a splendid Spring day and regardless of what you might have heard about April in Paris being unique and wonderful, after a long, hard winter there is a special aura to April in New York, too.

Godfrey could mingle easier in New York crowds than in other towns, so we strolled across 52nd Street over to Fifth with no interruptions. We went into the famous Mark Cross store where he wanted to select a gift.

After he had made his selection we moved down the aisle toward the cashier and ran head-on into Lucille Ball. She and Arthur knew each other from a couple of benefit shows on which they had appeared.

There were dual cries of recognition, a short chat and we all moved toward the cash register.

The young lady cashier heard the chatter and giddily called out to no one in particular, "Arthur Godfrey and Lucille Ball, the two redheads!!!"

From somewhere she produced a paper and pen and unprofessionally extended them, asking for their autographs. Both obliged and Arthur stood aside so Miss Ball could pay for her purchase.

The cashier rang up the purchases, added the New York sales tax and announced the total. By this time Miss Ball had extracted her charge card from her purse and handed it to the cashier.

Godfrey shook his head and chuckled when the young clerk, with the ink not yet dry on the autograph she had requested, examined the plastic card, turned to Miss Ball and asked "Do you have some form of identification?"

Arthur paid cash.

Twice, for about two years each time, Godfrey asked me to join his staff, ostensibly to advise him on public relations. He enjoyed a great popularity with millions of listeners across the country but occasionally his actions erupted into a firestorm of criticism. Godfrey always thought the press was unfair to him and this stirred up the passions of the multitudes.

The two most notable episodes were the firing on the air of singer Julius LaRosa, who had won a Talent Scouts show and been added to his morning show staff and the alleged buzzing of the control tower at Teterboro airport in New Jersey.

I was not around for either of these events but in his own mind Godfrey had been an unwilling victim of headline haters. He discussed with me both events in considerable detail and his explanations made a lot of sense to me.

When I joined Godfrey the first time, as he outlined my duties and responsibilities he was very candid. So was I.

"I have a pretty good sense of doing the right thing most of the time," Godfrey told me. "I think I'm right 90% of the time. That's high. Higher than most people, but that other 10% I can make a horrible mess of things."

"You will have a very easy job. If you can help me cut the 10% to 5%, I can handle the rest of it. Your job is easy – being right only half of the time," he concluded.

"To do that," I said, "I will need to have your full confidence and cooperation. If it's possible, I'd like for you to discuss with me anything you are going to do or say if it's something that might backfire into bad public relations."

"Hell," Arthur roared, "do you think I plan to do things that would cause the press to jump on me? I don't ever think what I am doing is unfair, unreasonable or should bring out reams of underserved criticism."

That was a brash request on my part, to ask the CBS star, who was unquestionably the most popular entertainer of his day, to share his agenda with a staff member, and a new one at that.

However, he agreed, to my satisfaction. Maybe it helped trim the boo-boos in half. Maybe we were just lucky that no P.R. blips appeared on the Godfrey screen during my times there.

The second time I came back into the Godfrey family was two years after I had formed the John Derr Company and had public relations clients in Washington, New York, Chicago and Los Angeles. I was also doing 15-18 golf tournament telecasts for CBS and the Hughes Network.

One of my clients was the General Electric Housewares Division, headed by Willard Sahloff, a big sports fan and also a Godfrey fan. This was important because if I was to add duties with Godfrey it had to be with GE's approval as they were my most financially rewarding client.

I told Arthur I could not help, even on a limited basis, unless GE agreed to share my time. When I broached the subject to Sahloff he said it might be possible and could help both clients but he would like to talk it over with Godfrey. He had never met Arthur and wanted to.

Setting up interviews for AG had been one of my responsibilities before so I knew how that could be done.

On the appointed day I accompanied Sahloff to CBS and did the introductions. You could tell by the second wave of conversation these two titans, one a big time entertainer and the other a successful manufacturer and both outstanding salesmen, were in sync. Easier than I had hoped.

I excused myself and left the two of them to decide the issue – would they find a compatible solution to let me retain both as clients? When I re-joined them half an hour later, one might have supposed they were life-long buddies.

Eventually Sahloff had to leave to return to his office in Bridgeport. No one mentioned my situation. Was I in or out? So I said to both, looking at neither, "what about my working arrangements?"

Godfrey looked at Sahloff, who returned the glance and said… "Oh, yes. That's what we were going to discuss. I have no problem. Let's leave it up to John and he'll find a way to work it out."

It was not very flattering to me that this summit meeting had lasted 45 minutes and not until it broke up did the reason for the meeting ever enter their discussion.

You might say Sahloff's concurrence served as my employment agreement. Godfrey chimed in with some affirmative reply and the meeting was over. A rather unusual way to be hired.

Four weeks later, Mary Ann Vann, Arthur's longtime capable private secretary, stopped me in the hall and said she was making up the payroll but didn't know what my retainer was.

Neither did I. "Mr. Godfrey doesn't know, either, but told me to ask you."

Into his office I went and repeated my conversation with Mary Ann. Godfrey agreed neither of us had mentioned money.

When he said: "Tell her to pay you what you think you are worth," I dusted off the old vaudeville joke and said, "No, I cant live on that."

Arthur smirked at the stale stab at humor, but when I mentioned a figure, all he said was... "tell Mary Ann." That trip doubled my salary.

Godfrey was a generous man. And kind. And thoughtful.

Before my days with him, a staff member from CBS Press Information had assisted in promoting his several shows. The young man, a friend of mine, was struck down by cancer and after an operation at Sloan-Kettering he returned to work. Not many months later the cancer returned and he passed away.

Godfrey liked the young man and knew he had bought a home in Westchester for his family that included eight children. His bank account was very slim, and now his widow was facing many new problems.

Godfrey and Ed Murrow had paid all the hospital charges but there were still those mortgage payments.

The day after the funeral AG ordered his lawyer to locate the mortgage and pay it in full. He then mailed the satisfied mortgage to the widow with the eight siblings. Godfrey's note to her expressed his sadness and said... "This is the least I can do. God bless you."

Individual Christmas gifts, usually good clothes, were sent each following year along with an envelope bearing each child's name. Inside was a $100 bill.

I learned of this generous gesture but I did not learn it from Godfrey. When I casually mentioned it to him one day, he looked sternly at me and said... "Yes, that's true. But don't you ever tell anyone about this. It's a matter between his family and me and not the business of anyone else..."

Then, as if to re-enforce his insistence on secrecy, he gave a negative wave of his hand and asked, "Do you understand?"

I said he was kind and considerate. This was not always his reputation to those who crossed him, but it was a side I saw, time after time.

Here's one episode to validate my opinion.

We had flown to St. Louis where Godfrey was giving his dressage performances with his Palomino stallion, Goldie. We were to be there six days, returning East on Sunday night in his customized Convair plane.

Sometime during the week I mentioned that my daughter, Cricket, would be seven years old on Thursday and this would be the first of her birthdays I had missed. It was not a big deal, just mentioned in our conversation.

AG said there's no need to miss it. "Call your wife and see if she and Cricket want to fly out here

Thursday afternoon. Frank (LaVigna, his pilot) can go back and pick them up at Teterboro and he can take them home Friday morning.

It was done.

Birthdays with Godfrey soon became old hat to her. The next November we were all in Toronto, where AG was appearing at the Royal Winter Fair.

Mary Ann called my room and told me Arthur was ready to leave for the Arena and would meet me in the lobby but he wanted to be sure Cricket was with me. He knew her fondness for horses and when we stepped out of the elevator, there stood Arthur holding a glazed clay vase, shaped like a horse's head and in it a corsage of flowers.

Cricket's eyes sparkled at the horse head vase and I doubt she heard the squeaky Godfrey baritone belting out "Happy Birthday." He was a caring man.

One of my assignments in India was to visit the Armed Forces rest camps up in the hill country and conduct "cracker barrel" sports talk sessions with the troops on leave from front-line duty in Burma and Assam.

General Joseph Stilwell, our theater commander, was himself an ardent sports fan and it was his contention that sports discussions were an excellent morale rejuvenator for those who were so far distant from their favorite playing fields and heroes.

In some theaters of war the USO arranged for sports and movie stars to visit and put on shows for the GIs. We had a few of these. Mostly they visited the European and Pacific war zones and skipped the China-Burma-India Theater. Even Bob Hope missed us. This void we filled by setting up our own sports rap sessions.

With troops from all parts of the USA and many with favorite sports and teams with which I was not familiar, it was necessary for me to line up Stateside writers and friends to send more sports news from home. I was more or less the moderator but it didn't take much to inspire these far from home soldier-fans to brag about their remembered heroes.

On one of my excursions to the camps I was told to travel by train to Kasali, the end of the rail line and stay a couple of nights at each of three camps in the area. Then I would be on my own for seven days until a new shipment of exhausted front-liners arrived for their two weeks of rest and relaxation.

It was during my seven-day break a friend and I decided to go north toward Tibet. I wanted to see Mt. Everest.

The only transportation would be by burro. We tried to rent a couple of burros but found out you had to buy the beast. Then if you returned it in good shape you could sell it back – for half what you paid for it.

Equipped with bed rolls, a stock of field rations and a map I had picked up from the Geodetic Survey office we bounced along the edge of town, settled in and headed north. With short but strong legs the burros moved at a steady pace.

We had no way of knowing how many miles we traveled that first day but it must have been about 40 before we unloaded, fed and tied the burros and slept under the stars.

During the night, clouds moved in and dawn was an overcast gray on our second day. Since it was not yet raining, we repacked and moved on up the narrow road. By our compass we were still headed north. Tibet and Everest were somewhere up ahead.

The rain began just before noon. Sometimes in India a rainstorm can last several days. Would this be that type rain, we wondered? The skies showed no sign of a let up, now so steady. We considered stopping but no tent, only our damp bed rolls, we could not raise much enthusiasm for making a mud pallet.

As darkness neared, up ahead and a 100 yards off our path there seemed to be a light. Perhaps a house, we thought. In the desert you often see a mirage but we were in the hilly, upcountry.

We steered our steeds toward the light. As we neared it we saw what appeared to us to be a mud hut with a thatched roof and no door. The light we saw was the flames from an open hearth fire shining through the open side of the hut.

Carefully we approached, calling out as we did. There was no answer. We moved on. We could see an Indian lady standing inside, with two small children clinging to her skirt behind her. Using a combination of English and Hindustani we tried to explain we were friendly travelers. It was evident she didn't understand.

Resorting to sign language we pointed to the falling rain and clutched our soaked clothing. She seemed to understand and did not object when we quietly moved inside. The warmth of the fire and shelter from the rain restored our bravado spirit.

We had miscalculated one thing. The lady was not the mother of the children. She was a nurse maid and while watching us she kept the two little toddlers a safe distance away. We had not figured that out until an Indian man and woman arrived. These were the parents and this lady understood English.

Again we explained who we were and where we were headed. Their friendliness was unexpected and most welcome.

Earlier my buddy and I had wondered if these children had ever seen a white person, since this was miles from any English settlement. Actually miles from any Indian villages.

We felt like real pioneers until we noticed over on what one might call the "landing" of the dirt stairs that led up about a half-flight to a low-ceilinged sleeping room – an outdated *LIFE Magazine*. What a surprise. We were still on planet earth even if the magazine was two years old.

This mystery was cleared up when we learned the mother had worked at an American hospital in Calcutta and when she returned to the hill country she had brought along this picture book from the hospital library. It contained the only pictures in the house and you could tell it had been looked at often.

With rain still falling the mother asked if we wanted to stay under shelter for the night. We put our bed rolls in the corner, safely away from the fire which they had stoked to burn all night. The Waldorf couldn't have been cozier.

After hot tea and what passed as an oaten cereal for breakfast, we said thanks to our new friends – the nicest people I ever had invited myself to visit – and again headed north.

In the far distance we could see mountains, the Himalayas, and that tallest, the one far to the right must be Mt. Everest. By now our narrow path became steeper and the burros took shorter steps. We paused more often...to rest and try to soothe our own painful posteriors. We had seen the mountains, including Mt. Everest, but they seemed so far away and the more we rode the more distant they appeared.

Nearer hills looked taller and blocked our view of Mt. Everest. Now no longer in sight, we had lost Mt. Everest. How could you lose something as big as Everest? We had.

About noon on the third day our path took us head-on into a river. There was no bridge and the banks were too steep to get down even if found a place to cross.

While the main path stopped abruptly at the river, a more narrow passageway went left and another went right, along the bank of the river. In addition to our maps we had inquired in Kasali about the route to Tibet or as near as we could get in the seven days available to us.

We had followed the route precisely but intervening hills now prevented us from seeing the tallest peaks and, we were unsure which path we should follow. If we could follow the river a few miles there might be an open plain that would give us a better look. But do we go right or left?

Since the river was flowing from left to right that would mean it started to our left as a mountain stream, so we took the left path. When, after about four miles, we still had no better view of Everest, I turned to my buddy, waved my hand across the sky and said, "Somewhere over there is Everest."

We turned the burros and headed home.

We had grossly miscalculated the distance.

Back in Kasali we sold the burros to the original owner, a snaggle-toothed merchant who paid us half of what we had paid him seven days earlier.

Confirming that our trip was successful, we asked why he had not told us which path to take at the river. He reasoned we would turn back before we ever reached the river. And then he let out a hearty laugh. I don't know if it was at our persistence or whether he was so pleased at having re-acquired his burrow...at a healthy profit.

Then he asked us which way we turned at the river. When we said we went left, his wrinkled face became a serious glint.

"Good thing for you," he said in his best attempt at English "If you go right a few miles, you in home country of Gurkhas...Head-hunting Gurkhas. Not so good for you."

Somewhere over there is Mt. Everest. I left it there.

And one night the Gurkhas went hungry. I left them too.

Have you ever noticed how golf pros, and I don't mean just the tour stars, but even club pros from around the country, will invariably open their conversation with... "How are you playing?"

Sam Snead was no different. Always when we met, the hello and handshake were immediately followed by "How are you playing?"

One time I recall making him listen to my answer.

"I'm playing well, that is, I'm playing a lot of holes well. Then for no reason I'll run into a bogey, double-bogey streak. There goes my score. Then maybe I'll par a few."

"You know what's wrong," Sam said, "you lose your concentration. You may hit a lazy shot or a careless shot. Then you try to recover but you are thinking about the shot you missed instead of concentrating on the upcoming shot. Losing your concentration is the surest way I know to ruin a score."

"How do you keep your concentration then?"

"Simple," Sam replied. "The next time you go out to play, tell yourself on the first hole that you are in sudden-death overtime. In sudden-death you must concentrate on every shot or the match may be over. There's no next hole to get even.

"Try that. Start off in sudden-death and

your concentration will not wander. Some folks can turn their concentration off and on at will. Demaret could do that. Hogan concentrated on every shot starting at the first tee. He'd smile a little smile, maybe shake hands and wish you good luck, but you can bet he already had locked in his concentrator.

"Play every hole like it's the last one. If you were really in sudden-death it might be."

If you have trouble concentrating, try Sam's method.

Snead had another choice bit of wisdom that might help you mentally and emotionally if you're having a bad day.

Another time, in answer to the usual greeting question, I cited another problem and no solution.

This time I said, "Sam, here lately I seem to be having an awful lot of bad breaks and it's got me down. If my ball is the least bit off line it winds up behind a tree or on the rocks or deepest rough of the course. These were not really bad shots – just bad results."

"I've had days like that myself," he said. "You can't do anything then about where the ball stops. It's there and you've got to play it. However, there is one thing you can do that can change your attitude.

"The next time you find your ball in one of these unfortunate locations, do this. You look

North and you look South. You look East and you look West.

"I guarantee you will see four worse places it could've been. Then play the lie you've got and quit complaining or thinking the breaks are going against you.

"It could have been worse, in at least four places."

_____

At the Meadowbrook club, during the Palm Beach Round-Robin, an overcast gray day prompted me to sympathize with Byron Nelson that the clouds were too bad for the golfers.

"Not at all, " Nelson avowed. "This is an ideal day for scoring....no winds, no shadows... gives us perfect depth deception."   Nelson shot 66 that day.

_____

"There is a sure way to know you are snatching away your club too fast, any club from driver to putter. Your club, on the takeaway, should leave your ball at the same speed that a ferry boat leaves the dock. It must be smooth and under control."

--Ben Hogan, once during lunchtime at Baltusrol Club in New Jersey.

_____

Branch Rickey, on assignment to comment on the World Series for Ed Murrow's CBS radio broadcast, was astounded when the Philadelphia catcher, after hitting an under-nourished drive toward shortstop, took four or five steps and stopped. He was returning to the bench when the ball was bobbled. The great Dodger executive turned toward me and said: "Lo, wherefor art thou, Seminick ? He had become a spectator." Rickey's tenet – "Never concede perfection to the opposition."

"Smoothness rather than speed is most important in the golf swing. There is nothing gained by swinging any club as hard as possible. With the putter too much speed can be fatal."
---Bob Jones

"If 'tis close enough to give, 'tis close enough to make". That's the way Laurie Auctorlonie, the Saint Andrews pro, answered a begging look for generosity from a member of our foursome one day on the course at Pinehurst. No, not me.

While awaiting the final putt, watching the CBS monitor,   Bob Jones was standing beside me as Jack Nicklaus was concluding another victory over Augusta National. He seemed unreal, prompting Mr. Jones to turn to me and say "He plays a game with which I am not familiar."

An outstanding gentleman, Don Padgett, former PGA president and the reclamation architect of the Pinehurst Resort, had this advice to young professionals, who sought his wisdom. "That was yesteryear. The things you did before today are done and gone. I like to look ahead, to see where I might make a difference in the future. Always look ahead."

"DON'T HIT IT"

You want a quick golf lesson from Bob Jones? Heed this:

One day in his years of failing health I stopped by Mr. Jones' law office in Atlanta for a short visit. The conversation got around to talking about golf commentary on television. Some of it he did not care for and in the privacy of his own office he bluntly assessed the lot.

"Bob, I'm sure I make some errors, too. Would you be kind enough sometime to jot down some notes that would help me be more accurate?"

"It's unlikely that I shall," he replied, "but you do use one word that has probably ruined more golf swings than any other in the history of the game."

That got my attention.

"What word is that?"

"I hear you say 'and here comes Boros and he's going to hit an 8 iron to the green'."

Becoming defensive, I quickly said we received much mail from viewers asking that we identify the clubs being used.

"That's not the problem," Jones said, with a wry smile, the ash falling from his elongated cigarette holder. You said he was HITTING an 8

348

iron. You don't hit an 8 iron... you PLAY an 8 iron.

"Just think about it for a minute," he said, leaning forward in his wheelchair. "The verb hit connotes furious action and while a lot of golf swings fall into that category, they shouldn't. When two cars run together you say they hit. And when they hit, they stop."

Jones slapped his fist into his hand, or as nearly as he could because of his crippled hand, but I got the point. He illustrated the hit...the collision...the stop.

"You play a golf stroke. You want the club to keep on moving after contact with the ball. In the process of playing the ball you complete your swing. That's what golf is all about.

"I'm told that 90% of those who play golf close their eyes at the moment of contact with the ball. Why? Well, it's because they are concerned about the savagery of that collision of the club versus the ball. They are thinking in terms of HIT when they should be relaxed and simply PLAY the ball.

"Tell your viewers to think of it as playing the ball...not hitting the ball. And while you are at it maybe you'd improve your game if you approached the ball less furiously."

Often, when talking to golf groups, they question me as to which of the 65 Masters I found most enjoyable. It's a fair question but an unfair answer. No two followed the same script. That's one of the charms of that tournament - you never know what to expect from whom.

For intrigue perhaps I would choose the 1968 Masters.

But first I take you back a week to the Greater Greensboro Open. At the GGO, Bob Goalby, a knowledgeable and well spoken professional, had been chosen to be our "guest analyst" on the telecast that week. Almost every week we brought a player up to my tower, outfitted him with head phones (which confused him), strapped on a microphone (which annoyed him), and discussed with him the actions we were seeing, hoping for some inside views.

On Thursday and Friday Bob climbed up to my tower at Sedgefield on the 17th fairway. Because of the terrain this was an unusually high platform. Normally about 20 feet up. This one was in the clouds and about 50 feet, a real tough climb. Bob was game and good.

Friday night was a terrible night. Martin Luther King was assassinated in neighboring Tennessee. There was an unrest throughout the nation and golf was not a priority. There was a request to cancel the tournament and the broadcast. This was refused. However, the television broadcast was scrubbed after threats were received demanding it.

Thus Goalby's debut was cancelled, however, we had spent two or three hours together on the early rounds, talking about golf, the coverage and the chance to get to know each other better.

Now move to Tuesday at Augusta National.

Naturally when I arrived I wanted to see how my frustrated tower assistant was playing. I first saw Bob as he was coming from the 18th green toward the club house.

"How did it go?"

Goalby said nothing for a moment, but his eyes scanned the whole area and sensing we were out of earshot, he said "I'm hitting it so good, I am afraid to quit. I have played 27 holes in practice and I am 13 under par."

Dinner had been scheduled with an old fiend from Etonic and when we met he asked if it was okay if he brought along another friend. Naturally not. I didn't know and didn't care. He was buying.

"Bob Goalby, one of our Etonic players, will join us then."

An omen, perhaps, it seemed.

Wednesday night at the CBS house, we were joined by the Sports Illustrated staff in our annual Calcutta party. The auctioneer was Bob Drum. With some 85 players in the field it was necessary to assemble the lesser knowns into fields or combinations for the big bids would go for Palmer, Nicklaus and Player. A secretary typed up the list of contestants, including venerable Jock Hutchinson and Fred McLeod, two octogenarians. As honorary starters they played nine holes.

Drum moved the Calcutta auction right along, but stopped for a nature break after an hour. During that break I, too cheap to ever wager on the players, carefully checked to see when my newest "best friend" might be up for bidding, not that I would buy him.

His name wasn't there. I asked Doc Giffen, of the Palmer tribe, to double check wth me. "Nope. There is no Goalby." I asked Giffen to say nothing and he would later know why.

Palmer was bid in. Then Nicklaus. And Drum announced the Calcutta was complete.

Hastily I raced up to the front. "Wait," I said. "We have two players that no one bought - McLeod and Hutchinson. I think they deserve a mention. I will bid $5 for McLeod and Hutchinson and anybody else not bid off."

The party was breaking up and the laughter was loud at Derr's foolish gesture. I explained my bet had Bob Goalby.

"No way..." they screamed. "Open up the bidding for Goalby." Bill MacPhail, who had succeeded me as head of the CBS Sports, ruled my bid was legitimate and I owned the three players, two of whom were going to play only nine holes. If that.

Now let's move to Sunday. The weather that year was wonderful and so was the golf. With 18 holes to go the lead belonged to Gary Player at 210. One stroke behind, at 211, came Don January, Bruce Devlin, Frank Beard , Raymond Floyd and Goalby.

Roberto deVicenzo began two behind Player, at 212, but he caught him on the first hole when his second shot found the cup for an eagle.

It was deVicenzo's 45th birthday and what a way to start. With birdies at 2,3 and 8, he was out in 31. DeVicenzo added birdies at 12 and 15 to lead by one, with still five players closing in. But here comes Goalby.

Birdies at 5,6, 8 marked Bob's card and then he rolled in another at the 13th, a par 5. And followed with another at the tough putting 14th, making four under for the day but still one behind the South American star, deVicenzo, whose four at 15 was another birdie, putting him 11 under.

DeVicenzo was three groups in front of Goalby. When Bob played a great second shot to the 15th, less than 12 feet away from an eagle, deVicenzo approached to three feet at 17.

In his CBS command truck, Producer/ Director Frank Chirkinian sensed they might be putting at the same moment, one at 15 for eagle, the other at 17 for birdie.

"John, we are going to split the screen and you will describe both of the putts from your tower. Watch the monitor so you can see. I think they may play at the same time."

We had never tried that exact scenario but here it comes. At 17, we saw Tommy Aaron step aside as Roberto settled over his putt. At 15, Goalby seemed in no hurry and as he rolled his in, so did Roberto. Both successful. Each 276.

I stayed on the tower to see another hole and saw they were tied. Then, Roberto missed the 18th green and bogeyed. Goalby three-putted 17, still knotted at 11 under par.

I walked up toward the clubhouse with Byron Nelson and I explained my Calcutta interest in the outcome. "Should I find who owns Roberto and offer to split?" I asked Nelson.

"No, you've come this far with Bob. Stay with him."

By the time we reached the clubhouse we heard the startling news that Roberto had signed for an incorrect 4 at No. 17, when all the television audience had seen him hole a birdie 3. Under the USGA rules, a higher score signed for becomes the accepted score, a lower score results in disqualification.

So Roberto became the runner-up, not through his play but because he accepted as correct the higher score entered by the player keeping score. He took total blame, but Mr. Roberts saw to it he received the identical trophy as Goalby, a marvelous silver rendition of the clubhouse.

That almost ends the 1968 tournament, except for one thing. MacPhail had held the pot. With little delay he handed over the first prize... $2,515.00. Not a bad investment of $5.

Our colleague Henry Longhurst reported this in his London Times column the next Sunday and with a further lamentation he added... "And wouldn't you know, he'd win it on a day when the pubs were closed."

It's an early ritual each morning to look out the western window of my second-floor bedroom in Maine to get an idea of what the weather this day might be. To look toward the mountains and the lake.

This morning something was missing.

The old elm tree that had stood just across the stone fence in the southwest corner of this clearing was crumpled. Its fragments lay on the ground.

From the window I could see that sometime in the darkness of night, silently for I had not heard it and I am a light sleeper, the ailing elm had given up the fight.

There was a time when there were other trees along the fence but for at least 80 years this elm had resisted all dangers -- the snows of winter, the blazing heat of summer and the frequent high winds that roared up the valley alongside Lake Kezar. It was the last. And it stood alone.

It had resisted quietly but successfully..

Some years ago the scrub trees that grow even among the hardy foes had been cleared out in order to get a better view of the waters of the lake. The underbrush have a way of coming back, stronger and bushier than ever.

That portion of the farm down the little road to the lake had been sold to a "flatlander" who did not realize trees need space to breathe too. The crowding was on his side of the stone fence as, in fact, was the stately elm, though just barely.

It may have been a dozen years ago when it became evident the tree was undergoing stress. Yes, trees have stress, too. It started in the lower branches, not the top as one might imagine. The leaves were smaller and sometimes misshapen as though a moth or other creatures were eating them. They probably were.

This told me the trees needed help. A forester friend told me trees also suffer from stress and the old elm, crowded by saplings was in need of help. My neighbor felt differently. He had the tree. I had the view.

But each spring, the new leaves would freshen the world with a greenery that could only be an elm's new dress. And when I saw that I thought maybe the old gal was going to make it another season.

If you wonder why I spoke of the elm as a "her", I said the new dress was green and clean and only ladies wear dresses like that.

Then this spring when I arrived, it was evident the winter had done the old elm no favor. Not so much the cold, but perhaps the chilly winds had pierced the aging bark and weakened the fiber of the limbs. And I knew that one day soon, the damaged limbs would give way, reducing the tree to the nakedness of a sentinel, a tree that had once bushed out in symmetrical solarity, a tree in a row of trees. Now it stood alone.

It was that aloneliness that captivated me.

Other trees that used to stand in that row of elms along the western stone wall had yielded to the inevitable. They were gone. Visitors who had never seen them did not miss them. I did. And I cherished the lone survivor .

That's also the way I felt about this beautiful lake that lies just down the hill. It is hidden by scrubs and tall pine trees. These would be healthier if thinned. Late in the afternoon from my porch I can see the shimmering sunshine on the water as it bolts its way through the forest and into my view .

That view is gone.

Now the old elm is gone. Around the shattered stump lie the broken limbs, evidence that from time to time one and then another fell to the ground. Left standing was the barkless trunk.

And this morning even the trunk has tumbled.

Life is like the elm it seems. There is a time of growing. Then a time of growing up. And later a time of growing old. Then one day the trunk falls too.

Goodbye, old elm.. Whether male or female, I loved you. And without you or me, life will go on.

GOODBYE.